SO-FQV-560

Headline Series

No. 281   FOREIGN POLICY ASSOCIATION $4.00

REFORMING THE INTERNATIONAL MONETARY SYSTEM

From Roosevelt to Reagan

by Robert D. Hormats

Cover Design: Hersch Wartik

Nov./Dec. 1986
Published June 1987

The Author

ROBERT D. HORMATS is Vice-President of Goldman Sachs & Co. and Director of Goldman Sachs International Corp. He was appointed Assistant Secretary of State for Economic and Business Affairs by President Reagan (1981–82); he had previously served as a member of the National Security Council staff (1969–76) and as Deputy Assistant Secretary of State for Economic and Business Affairs (1977–79). He was appointed Deputy U.S. Trade Representative, with the rank of ambassador, by President Carter (1979–81).

Mr. Hormats has a Ph.D. in international economics from the Fletcher School of Law and Diplomacy at Tufts University, has been guest lecturer at Princeton University, has written extensively on international economics and foreign policy and is the recipient of the French Legion of Honor.

This work is dedicated to my parents, Ruth and Saul Hormats.

The Foreign Policy Association
The Bretton Woods Committee

This publication is a joint effort of the Foreign Policy Association and the Bretton Woods Committee. FPA is a private, nonprofit, nonpartisan educational organization whose purpose is to stimulate wider interest and more effective participation in world affairs. The Bretton Woods Committee is a nonprofit organization that promotes discussion of issues related to U.S. support for the International Monetary Fund and the World Bank.

The author is responsible for factual accuracy and for the views expressed in the HEADLINE SERIES. FPA itself takes no position on issues of U.S. foreign policy.

HEADLINE SERIES (ISSN 0017-8780) is published five times a year, January, March, May, September and November, by the Foreign Policy Association, Inc., 205 Lexington Ave., New York, N.Y. 10016. Chairman, Robert V. Lindsay; President, John W. Kiermaier; Editor in Chief, Nancy L. Hoepli; Senior Editor, Ann R. Monjo; Associate Editor, K. M. Rohan. Subscription rates, $15.00 for 5 issues; $25.00 for 10 issues; $30.00 for 15 issues. Single copy price $4.00. Discount 25% on 10 to 99 copies; 30% on 100 to 499; 35% on 500 to 999; 40% on 1,000 or more. Payment must accompany order for $8 or less. Add $1 for postage. Second-class postage paid at New York, N.Y. POSTMASTER: Send address changes to HEADLINE SERIES, Foreign Policy Association, 729 Seventh Ave., New York, NY 10019. Copyright 1987 by Foreign Policy Association, Inc. Composed and printed at Science Press, Ephrata, Pennsylvania.

Library of Congress Catalog Card No. 87-80815
ISBN 0-87124-113-7

Preface

When I was asked to write this book in the fall of 1985, the search was just beginning for ways to improve, or replace, the floating rate international monetary system—or nonsystem, as its critics charge. The era of floating currencies had begun in 1973. It was heralded at the time as a more market-oriented successor to the fixed-but-adjustable exchange rate system embodied in the 1944 Bretton Woods agreements. As time went on, however, floating rates came to be associated with international imbalances and instability. It is a matter of debate whether such problems were primarily the result of the new exchange rate system, of economically disruptive political developments (such as the Middle East war of October 1973 and the 1979 overthrow of the shah of Iran, which led to major oil shocks), or of inappropriate domestic policies. Every observer can apportion fault differently. But even if one does not blame the current exchange rate system for the major part of the world's economic ills, as its harshest detractors indeed do, most observers are likely to agree that it has not worked nearly as well as its original advocates had predicted.

The central international institution in the world monetary system is the International Monetary Fund. Its role has changed substantially over the years, but it is certainly no less important today than 43 years ago when it was established. Indeed the IMF now has a considerably broader and more significant function in the world economy than when it was launched. Its initial mission was to finance temporary balance-of-payments deficits. Over the years it added the role of actively encouraging improvements in domestic policies in order to maintain balance-of-payments equilibrium. More recently it has been supporting efforts of developing countries to overcome unsustainable debt burdens.

This book examines the changed, and changing, international

monetary system. It describes how the system has evolved under nine Presidents—from Franklin D. Roosevelt to Ronald Reagan. It also discusses the broader evolution of the world economy during this period, including the trade and investment issues to which international monetary policy is closely linked.

The subjects to be considered, although predominantly international, have a major impact on domestic economies. And, in the final analysis, that is why they concern most Americans. The dollar's exchange rate has an enormous effect on U.S. factory workers, farmers, corporate managers and bankers, as well as on every American who buys a car, a television set, a bottle of wine or any other good which is imported or must compete with imports. No one in the United States, or in any other country, is immune from the impact of the dollar's exchange rate or from the uncertainty surrounding its future value. Because of its pervasive and dominant role in the international economy, the American dollar is international as well as national money. Achieving improved currency stability and alignment is of increasing importance to the United States today because dollar volatility can disrupt large portions of the U.S. economy.

Just as Americans insist that the cars and computers they buy work well, so should they urge sound policies and effective institutions to keep the dollar stable and in line with market fundamentals. But since the dollar is part of a wide network of global financial and commercial relationships, its stability can only be achieved in an international context. Cooperation among the major countries, not unilateral action, is the only logical and sustainable way of making the exchange rate system work better and of fostering a healthy international economy.

Progress cannot be made through ad hoc measures. The IMF and groups operating within its framework are likely to continue to play essential roles in the process of international monetary cooperation and in the effort to improve world monetary arrangements. The effective functioning of the IMF will continue to be necessary to support sound domestic economic policies, ease the Third World debt problem, and maintain currency rates that facilitate the orderly flow of finance and trade.

1

The Bretton Woods System

In 1944 representatives of the United States, Britain and 42 other nations agreed on a plan to create a new international monetary system designed to stabilize exchange rates,* restore the convertibility of currencies suspended by World War II, and thus foster increased world trade. It was the first step toward reconstruction of the world economy following the war.

Forty years after that historic meeting at Bretton Woods, New Hampshire, another conference was held at that same spot. A few who took part in the original meeting attended. They mingled and exchanged observations with those responsible for the functioning of the present, vastly different system. It was a moving moment for all of us who had the privilege to participate—not only because of the historic dimensions of what those remarkable founders had achieved four decades ago, but also because of the palpable awareness at this Bretton Woods conference that vision and leadership were required anew to improve a system now in disrepute.

It is too easy to lose sight of the significance of the 1944 Bretton Woods agreements because the exchange rate regime they created

*Glossary of terms used throughout begins on page 77.

July 1944: Delegates from more than 40 countries attending the monetary conference at Bretton Woods, N.H.

faltered and ultimately collapsed in the early 1970s. Bretton Woods was a historic achievement. The International Monetary Fund (IMF, or the Fund) and the International Bank for Reconstruction and Development (World Bank)—the latter created at the same conference in order to provide loans to rebuild nations devastated by war and to assist developing countries—are lasting, impressive and still vital monuments to their architects.

The period between World War I and World War II had been one of international economic chaos characterized by competitive currency devaluations, discriminatory restrictions on trade and a plethora of other beggar-thy-neighbor policies. The participants at Bretton Woods agreed on a system designed to avoid a repeat performance. President Franklin D. Roosevelt saw the Bretton Woods agreements as necessary to prevent a return to the economic deterioration and friction that had helped lead to World War II. In urging congressional passage of legislation to imple-

Delegates and their advisers in attendance at a session of the Bretton Woods conference in the Mount Washington Hotel

ment the agreements, he emphasized that "exchange rates must be stabilized and the channels of trade opened up throughout the world. . . .The world will either move toward unity and widely shared prosperity or it will move apart into necessarily competing economic blocs." Roosevelt's secretary of state Cordell Hull echoed these sentiments. In the past "unhampered trade dovetailed with peace; high tariffs, trade barriers and unfair economic competition, with war."

The basic operating principle of the Bretton Woods agreements was that countries should try to conduct domestic economic policies so as to keep their exchange rates stable, fixed at set parities. Thus, governments agreed in advance that, say, one British pound should equal $2.80, and committed themselves to maintain that exchange rate. Exchange rates were, in effect, the parameters within which domestic policy was to operate. If differing amounts of inflation, economic growth or levels of interest rates led to upward or downward pressures on exchange parities, domestic policies were to be changed to reduce such pressures, while exchange rates remained at their preset levels.

The architects of the Bretton Woods agreements also aimed at achieving convertibility among currencies when they were used to make payments for trade in goods and services, that is, transactions on current account. Insistence on currency stability and convertibility was an attempt to avert the trade and financial distortions that had resulted in the interwar period from the widespread use of foreign exchange restrictions and trade discrimination.

Dealing with Imbalances

The participants at Bretton Woods also recognized that from time to time nations would encounter serious balance-of-payments surpluses or deficits that would put pressures on exchange rate parities. A country with a severe trade deficit, for example, would suffer a net outflow of its currency. The resulting international oversupply would exert downward pressure on the value of the currency, forcing the government concerned to intervene, purchasing its own currency in the foreign exchange market with its reserves of foreign currencies. In so doing it would attempt to prevent its own currency from falling in value vis-à-vis other currencies. A country which ran low on the foreign currency needed to undertake successful intervention or to maintain a reasonable level of imports was permitted to "draw" on a pool of resources held by the IMF (resources composed of members' contributions of gold, dollars and other currencies).

The architects of the Bretton Woods system recognized that there would be times when a country's payment imbalance was likely to be long-lasting; in IMF terms, the country would then be in "fundamental disequilibrium." If a country suffered from a large and apparently long-lived current account deficit (a deficit on trade and services combined), its drawings from the IMF to defend its currency's existing exchange rate would soon reach the limits permitted under IMF rules. In the process, the country undoubtedly would also have used up substantial amounts of its own reserves. If the IMF found such a country to be in fundamental disequilibrium, it would sanction a specific devaluation—a lowering of the worth in terms of gold—of the country's currency.

The architects of Bretton Woods understood, however, that the IMF was to be an instrument for achieving monetary stability and convertibility in reasonably normal conditions—not for promoting reconstruction in war-torn countries. At the same time, the Fund could not achieve its monetary goals if, as was then the case, the United States had the lion's share of world productive capacity and world liquidity, with its plentiful gold reserves and the extremely high international acceptance of the dollar.

To support postwar recovery, the Bretton Woods conference established the World Bank, with an authorized capital of $10 billion. Most of this amount was quickly lent to Western Europe to rebuild its economic infrastructure. But Europe's prodigious demand for goods and capital equipment proved far greater than World Bank resources could satisfy. In the late 1940s, Europe ran large balance-of-payments deficits and soon depleted its reserves of foreign exchange and gold.

To help restore economic and monetary balance, the United States provided substantial aid and financing to Western Europe. President Harry S. Truman gave large-scale aid to Greece and Turkey and later launched the remarkably successful Marshall Plan. In four years, more than $13 billion in vitally needed U.S. assistance was extended to Western Europe under the plan. The U.S. military presence added another important source of funds to Western European economies.

The dollar was the "key" currency in the world monetary system. The United States undertook to fix the dollar-gold relationship at $35 to one troy ounce of gold: were a foreign central bank to present $35 to the U.S. Treasury, it would receive an ounce of gold in return. Other countries, in conjunction with the IMF, would determine how much gold each of their currencies was to be worth. If, for instance, one dollar was to be worth four West German marks (deutsche marks), and one dollar was to be worth 1/35 of an ounce of gold, then one deutsche mark would be worth $1/140$ of an ounce of gold. But only the dollar, the key currency, was directly convertible into gold.

The key-currency role for the dollar turned out to be a flaw in the system. A large increase in the holdings of dollars abroad (both in absolute terms and relative to the U.S. gold stock) ultimately undermined the credibility of, and finally helped to destroy, the Bretton Woods system. It led to growing doubts that the United States could honor its commitment to convert dollars into gold.

A second major flaw was the lack of clear guidelines regarding upward changes in exchange rates. There was no way to compel countries with chronic, large current account surpluses to raise the exchange rate of their currencies to help reduce these surpluses. Most countries in such a position did not want to see the increase in imports and decrease in exports—and perhaps slower domestic growth rates—that would result from a higher currency value. This reluctance meant that the system tended to force a greater degree of the "adjustment" burden on countries suffering from current account deficits than on countries with current account surpluses. In short, there was a lack of symmetry in the IMF system. In the quarter century following the establishment of the Bretton Woods system, only four increases in exchange rate parity occurred; there were over 100 reductions.

The system also tended to be very rigid. When people engaged in trading foreign exchange perceived that a country was in fundamental disequilibrium, they usually anticipated an exchange rate devaluation. In this relatively riskless situation, they speculated against the country's currency. Pressures thus built up on the currency, increasing the likelihood that it would have to be devalued.

Steady Dollar Outflow

Over time the system became increasingly vulnerable to these flaws. After the war the United States, in effect, assumed the role of a global central bank by supplying the rest of the world with dollars. Its balance-of-payments deficits, due largely to loans and grants to other governments and to military expenditures abroad, resulted in a steady outflow of dollars. The dollar outflow was especially high in 1957 and 1958. That outflow increased the foreign exchange reserves of Western Europe, Japan and other countries recovering from the war.

For several years after the war, many observers believed that because the United States had most of the world's productive capacity, other countries could not hope to compete with it and thus would constantly need to borrow dollars. As time went on, this view began to change. Confidence abroad grew as Western European nations rebuilt their economies, increased their exports and gained dollars.

In the postwar years most Western European countries maintained currency inconvertibility to husband their dollar reserves. By 1958, they had sufficient reserves to make their currencies convertible. That paved the way for large American investment in Western Europe, because foreign currencies earned from such investment could now be converted back into dollars. (Japan took a similar step in 1964.) By 1960, U.S. private capital flows to Western Europe reached over $1.5 billion—compared with an average of something over $400 million in the three previous years.

The outflow of dollars resulting from the factors noted above led to a buildup of dollars in foreign hands. In 1960 European and Japanese reserves together exceeded those of the United States: total holdings of dollars abroad roughly equaled U.S. gold reserves. This cast doubt on the ability of the U.S. Treasury to convert dollars into gold if foreign central banks should wish to convert substantial sums.

The United States sought means to stem the dollar outflow. President Dwight D. Eisenhower took the payments imbalance very much into account in submitting a surplus budget for 1960 and in ordering his treasury secretary to negotiate an "offset" agreement with West Germany. Under the agreement, West Germany accepted the obligation to help defray the cost of American soldiers stationed there. The United States took other steps. It ordered U.S. foreign aid to be used to make purchases from the United States insofar as possible. It recalled dependents of U.S. forces abroad. It began insisting on a greater opening of Western European markets to American exports. And the U.S. Federal Reserve Board (the Fed), for the first time, decided to participate in meetings of the Bank for International Settlements (BIS) at Basel, Switzerland. Western European central bankers met there regularly with a view to maintaining stable currencies. Previously the United States had shunned the BIS as a European "club." Later, during the 1960s, the BIS, with U.S. support, played a major role in supporting the British pound and the Italian lira and in stabilizing the price of gold on world markets.

President John F. Kennedy was highly preoccupied with the U.S. balance-of-payments deficit and its implications for international financial stability. Arthur M. Schlesinger Jr. recounts that in the early 1960s, "Kennedy. . .used to tell his advisers that the two things which scared him most were nuclear war and the payments deficit." And he called the 35:1 dollar-gold relationship "the foundation stone of the free world's trade and payments system." Kennedy also noted, however, that "it may not always be desirable or appropriate to rely entirely" on increases in the supply of gold, dollars or other currencies to satisfy the requirements of the nations of the world for additional reserves. He asked for an international study of how "international monetary institutions—especially the IMF—can be strengthened and more effectively utilized. . .in furnishing needed increases in reserves." But there was little time in the short-lived Kennedy Administration to devise new means of creating reserves.

In the early 1960s, the United States and Western Europe began a monetary debate which, in one form or other, has continued to this day. At first, the Europeans accused the United States of exporting inflation by pursuing an excessively expansionary monetary policy at home. This, they argued, led to low interest rates in the United States and an outflow of U.S. capital to Europe, where it could earn higher rates of interest. The United States claimed that Europeans were pursuing monetary policies that were too tight, which resulted in high interest rates that encouraged the movement of dollars to Europe. The United States and Western Europe traded demands—not unlike those of today—that the other adjust domestic policies to reduce the payments imbalance between the two. The lack of symmetry in IMF rules, referred to earlier, and the lack of specifics for determining how adjustment should take place, began to emerge as problems.

Worry About Gold

A related worry had to do with the dollar-gold relationship. Concerns grew that the desire of some private individuals to hold gold as a hedge against inflation or dollar devaluation would lead to an increase in its price on the free market. In effect this would mean a devaluation of the dollar vis-à-vis gold. And it would give rise to speculation regarding an *official* dollar devaluation, which most countries wanted to avoid because a large portion of their reserves was held in dollars. Moreover, any substantial change in the then sacrosanct dollar-gold relationship—Kennedy's "foundation stone"—raised the specter of major disruptions in the world financial system.

The United States was especially fearful that an increase in the free-market price of gold, say to $40 to one ounce, would convince the world that an official dollar devaluation vis-à-vis gold was on the way. Such a conviction could not only increase private speculation but also could lead to a rush by foreign central banks on the U.S. Treasury to buy gold at $35 an ounce. A rush of this kind could force the Treasury to stop converting dollars into gold for fear of running U.S. gold reserves down too far.

In light of these concerns, in 1960 the United States and seven of its principal economic partners agreed to sell gold from their reserves on the free market to prevent a large price increase. This procedure was later formalized by creation of the so-called gold pool to support the existing dollar-gold relationship.

2

Cracks in the System

Britain's financial problems in the 1960s foreshadowed those that emerged in the United States in the 1970s. Strong British economic growth in the early 1960s led to a surge in imports and eventually to a deterioration in Britain's current account balance. Foreign central banks with large holdings of the pound sterling grew nervous and started selling. A high rate of inflation in Britain further raised concerns about Britain's ability to sustain the pound at its postwar rate of $2.80. Despite major efforts to maintain the value of the pound, Britain was under enormous pressure to devalue.

A devaluation of sterling was seen by some as necessary to improve the country's trade performance and to stem speculation against the pound. But the idea was controversial at that time. Many took the very mention of devaluation as a sign of the decline in Britain's role and strength in the world economy. (A similar psychology led many Americans to resist passionately the devaluation of the dollar in the early 1970s.) But there were other reasons for reluctance to see the pound devalued.

Devaluation would constitute a loss for those nations, particularly in the British Commonwealth, that held the pound in their reserves. And because the pound was the only major world reserve currency apart from the dollar, the United States was concerned that devaluation would trigger speculation against the dollar. That, in turn, could prompt many governments to buy gold from the U.S. Treasury, or private individuals to buy more gold on the free market. Such moves would weaken the credibility of the U.S. gold-convertibility guarantee. Finally, the United States believed that the devaluation of the pound would ultimately weaken U.S. competitiveness, because exports from Britain and from countries whose currencies were tied to the pound would become cheaper.

Britain faced a major currency crisis in 1961 as the pound fell in world markets. The size of intervention in foreign exchange markets in order to support the pound's value exceeded funds available to Her Majesty's Treasury. Consequently, an ad hoc package of loans in currencies suitable for intervention had to be improvised by the U.S. Federal Reserve and other central banks. In the face of this massive sterling defense effort, the crisis subsided.

In order to address this problem, and similar problems in the future, the 10 major industrialized nations created a special facility—the General Arrangements to Borrow (GAB)—to which they pledged up to $6 billion. Although these funds were to be available to the IMF in an emergency to lend to countries to bolster their intervention efforts, they could be used only with the consent of the 10 contributors. Later, the same group of countries, which came to be called the Group of Ten, expanded its role from merely overseeing the GAB; it became the main forum for discussing reform of the international monetary system.

A Time of Turbulence

Pressures on the pound resumed in mid-1967. By November 1967, after massive sales of that currency in private foreign exchange markets, and futile intervention by central banks, the pound had to be devalued—from $2.80 to $2.40. Bretton Woods was beginning to crumble.

Following devaluation of the pound, sales from the gold pool were required to prevent the gold price from rising on the free market in terms of dollars. The United States, to strengthen confidence in the dollar, sought to improve its balance-of-payments position. President Lyndon B. Johnson, backed by Federal Reserve Board Chairman William McChesney Martin, pledged not to change the 35:1 dollar-gold conversion rate. He also launched a number of programs aimed specifically at ending the U.S. balance-of-payments deficit. And he placed severe limits on investment abroad by Americans to curtail the further outflow of funds from the United States.

As the 1960s drew to a close, turbulence in foreign exchange markets intensified and currency volatility became widespread. In Europe, the exchange rate between the French franc and West German mark became subject to intense speculative activity. The 1968 civil disturbances in France, known as the events of May, led to downward pressure on the franc. The same year saw upward pressure on the West German mark resulting from that country's impressive trade performance. During 1969, President Georges Pompidou of France, in a move that surprised many because it was not the result of a run on the franc at the time, devalued his nation's currency. Subsequently, West Germany reacted to further upward pressure by letting the deutsche mark "float" for a time, allowing its price to be set by market forces. The West Germans then revalued the mark at roughly 9 percent above its previous parity.

Although at the time observers recognized that something fundamental was wrong, the debate over improving the international monetary system during the 1960s concentrated largely on only one of the major flaws of the system—the composition and adequacy of international reserves. The debate virtually ignored the lack of rules for changing exchange rate parities or reducing current account imbalances by other means. The concentration of attention on reserves reflected the still widely accepted notion that fixed rates should be preserved. Thus the major focus of reform was not on rules for rational changes in parities, but on how countries could obtain sufficient financial resources to maintain existing parities.

16

The effort to improve the methods by which the system created and distributed reserves was given impetus by the recognition of Americans and non-Americans alike that the world could not continue to rely heavily or indefinitely on dollars to increase its total reserves. Countries such as France did not want to permit the United States the luxury of a system in which other nations held dollars in virtually unlimited amounts, which President Charles de Gaulle had termed an "exorbitant privilege." This system, French officials argued, permitted the United States to escape economic discipline and avoid pressures to reduce its large balance-of-payments deficit. France reasoned that if the United States were forced to convert foreign-held dollars into gold or other currencies, Washington would abandon those policies which led to the excessive outflow of dollars.

Birth of the SDR

A series of negotiations was conducted in the 1960s, primarily by the Group of Ten, to create some type of new reserve asset. France, in these negotiations, favored elevating the role of gold. In part this reflected the French desire to reduce the dollar's privileged role; in part it reflected a historic French confidence in gold. In any case, France's two reasons were consistent. Paris correctly perceived that under some circumstances a greater role for gold in the system vis-à-vis the dollar would impose more discipline on the United States. If, for example, the United States were to be forced to provide gold to replace a great many of the dollars in the world's reserves, it would have to take measures to reduce its payments deficit.

The United States wanted reforms that would not lead to an elimination or sharp curtailment of the ability of other nations to hold dollars as reserves. In July 1965, with the authorization of President Johnson, Secretary of the Treasury Henry Fowler announced the willingness of the United States to negotiate the creation of a supplementary reserve asset to make the availability or liquidity of international reserves less dependent on both the dollar and gold. The result was the Special Drawing Right (SDR), which was ultimately agreed upon in 1968 after prolonged negotiations. The SDR was nicknamed "paper gold" because it was designed to play a reserve role similar to that of gold. In this sense, the establishment of SDRs, which were created by a stroke of the pen on the books of the IMF, was a historic step that would permit conscious decisions by the Fund to create more reserve assets. In the future, world liquidity was no longer to be totally dependent on the output of gold mines in South Africa and the Soviet Union, or on continued U.S. balance-of-payments deficits that supplied the world with dollars. President Johnson praised the SDR agreement for creating an instrument which "can meet the future needs of the world for international liquidity—in the proper amounts and in a usable form."

Thereafter, at least in principle, whenever it became necessary to increase world liquidity, the IMF could create and allocate SDRs. Each member of the IMF would receive a percentage of the overall SDR issue comparable to its quota in the IMF. A country's quota—and therefore also its share of SDR allocation—is based roughly on its relative share of world gross national product (GNP).

Under the SDR mechanism, a country needing foreign currencies to defend its exchange rate would simply transfer SDRs from its account at the Fund to the account of another country. In exchange it would receive that country's currency, which it would then use to buy its own currency in foreign exchange markets, thereby raising market demand. This would prevent its currency from declining too sharply in value. The first allocation of SDRs was made on January 1, 1970.

While helping at the margin to increase liquidity in the international monetary system, creation of the SDR has done little to reduce the central role of the dollar. Too few SDRs have been created to make a major difference. Governments of the United States and West Germany have been apprehensive about the inflationary consequences of large increases in SDRs. And smaller countries, by insisting on very large SDR issues, have created the impression that they see them as a form of aid to bolster ailing economies.

Fixed Rates Stay Fixed

Although agreement was reached on the SDR, little progress was made on how to deal with increasing pressures on exchange rates. Many economists were reluctant to entertain the notion that there could be any monetary system other than one built around fixed rates, the anchor and major source of economic discipline for many economies. And the U.S. commitment to preserving the dollar's relationship to gold came to be a compelling factor in U.S. domestic economic policy. President Kennedy's February 6, 1961, message to the Congress had stressed that "The United States must, in the decades ahead, much more than at any time in the past, take its balance of payments into account when formulating its economic policies and conducting its economic affairs." In July 1963, the Federal Reserve raised its discount rate in order to stem the outflow of capital from the United States and thus avert a threat to the dollar. In 1968, with the dollar under heavy downward pressure following the devaluation of the British pound, Congress sought to limit Federal expenditures to stop the slide. Arthur M. Okun, then economic adviser to President Johnson, stated that "the threat of international financial crisis may well have been the single most decisive factor in getting Congress to move on fiscal restraint."

Exchange rate discipline was also important abroad. In 1966, the British government under Prime Minister Harold Wilson fashioned a number of extremely tough measures to raise taxes and curtail consumer credit, as well as freeze wages and prices, in order to strengthen sterling. France took similar steps to defend the franc in 1968. Capital controls were from time to time applied toward similar ends in Britain, France and other countries, including the United States.

However, there were limits to the willingness of nations to subject their economies to discipline induced by the need to preserve existing currency relationships. Without a set of guidelines for determining when and how countries in fundamental disequilibrium—especially countries in chronic, large surplus— were to adjust their exchange rates or otherwise reduce their imbalances, major tensions built up in the system.

With the devaluation of the pound in 1967, the first major jolt to the system, the debate over how to improve the adjustment process began in earnest. As the decade wore on and the Vietnam War led to high government deficits, inflation and large expenditures abroad, the U.S. balance-of-payments position weakened. Observing this, many Americans came to believe it unfair for other countries to devalue their currencies, or maintain them at undervalued levels, while the United States was committed both to maintain a fixed dollar-gold relationship and to guarantee the dollar's convertibility into gold.

By 1969-70, as today, the United States was beginning to seek external help to improve its balance-of-payments position. It demanded a major international currency realignment. More fundamentally, it also wanted to eliminate the flaws in the monetary system that permitted prolonged currency misalignments. U.S. officials believed that the system itself impaired the adjustment process and therefore imposed an obstacle to America's ability to compete in the world. Then, as now, the surpluses of Japan and West Germany were seen as problems. Then, as now, the question of how to induce surplus countries to adjust was seen as important. Then, as now, other nations attributed the U.S. payments deficit primarily to America's own domestic economic policies.

3

The Camp David Bombshell
and the Move toward Floating Rates

When Richard M. Nixon assumed the presidency in January 1969, consensus was building in favor of some change in the exchange rate system. The IMF at the time was considering wider "bands" for fluctuations in currency rates. The original fixed rate system permitted a small amount of movement above or below the fixed, or parity, rate. The margin on either side of parity within which the exchange rate was permitted to fluctuate was called the band. The IMF was also considering means of encouraging prompter adjustments in currency values, rather than waiting until changes were forced by large imbalances in a nation's international transactions. It even contemplated the use, from time to time, of a temporary period of floating to enable a currency to find a more market-related exchange rate (drawing on the then recent West German experience with a short float).

By 1971, pressures on the United States had become more urgent and more political. Its concerns were not so much about the technicalities of exchange rate reform as about explicit exchange rate realignment. The U.S. balance of merchandise trade, for the first time since World War II, had moved into deficit in mid-1971, sparking domestic demands for protection against imports and for an exchange rate which would improve U.S. competitiveness. The major question was how to achieve the latter. The dollar was tied to gold at a specific price, and thus "permanently" fixed. Meanwhile, other currencies could move up or down vis-à-vis the dollar. Even if the United States attempted to devalue the dollar vis-à-vis gold and other currencies to improve U.S. international competitiveness, other nations could simply offset the benefits for the United States by devaluing *their* currencies by a similar amount.

For a time the United States, recognizing the constraints on its ability to devalue the dollar, and reflecting domestic opposition to doing so, pressed surplus countries to revalue their currencies. The West German revaluation had encouraged the United States to believe that in the future surplus countries would more readily permit appreciation of their currencies. But for the most part U.S. trading partners enjoyed having large trade surpluses and were reluctant to risk losing them by revaluing. Many also argued that it was largely U.S. policies that had created U.S. trade deficits and thus it was the responsibility of the United States to change such policies. Europeans were reluctant to stimulate their economies to draw in more U.S. goods or to raise the value of their currencies, construing such measures as "letting the United States off the hook."

At the end of 1969 the author had just arrived in Washington as a very junior member of the National Security Council staff. The economic section was then under the able leadership of C. Fred Bergsten. The author can vividly recall the anguished debates in Washington at that time on how to encourage other nations to revalue their currencies. Their resistance to doing so was intense, and there were dire predictions of the great catastrophe that would surely befall the international financial system if the United States took the initiative by devaluing the dollar vis-à-vis gold.

A Resort to 'Floats'

During 1969 and 1970, West Germany as well as Canada and the Netherlands had floated their currencies rather than try to defend rates that, because the market considered them too low, were the target of powerful speculative activity. West Germany, in particular, had been forced to purchase large amounts of dollars in order to prevent a major appreciation of the deutsche mark vis-à-vis the dollar; the float relieved it of this requirement. The Netherlands, with its currency closely linked to the deutsche mark, floated the guilder. Both West Germany and the Netherlands refixed at a higher exchange rate in a few weeks. Canada, at the time enjoying a strong current account position and large capital inflow, decided on a floating dollar rather than continue to buy U.S. dollars in the market.

These developments helped to dampen the speculative pressures of the time. But in mid-1971, there was new turbulence resulting in downward pressure on the U.S. dollar and upward pressure on the deutsche mark, guilder, Swiss franc and yen. Concerns about the U.S. trade deficit, U.S. inflation and low interest rates relative to those abroad, as well as a congressional report stating that the dollar should be devalued, had caused enormous capital outflows from the United States. Although there were few requests by foreign central banks to convert their dollar holdings—some of them considerably enlarged by recent intervention in currency markets—into gold, apprehensions grew in Washington that there could be a run on U.S. gold reserves.

Action at Camp David

President Nixon, who along with his treasury secretary John Connally was given to bold strokes, decided to deal with a number of problems at the same time: a U.S. inflation rate in excess of 4 percent, increasing domestic unemployment and the U.S. trade deficit. These difficulties induced Nixon to take a comprehensive and strong set of measures. At a meeting at Camp David on August 15, 1971, the President decided to impose a 10 percent surcharge on U.S. imports and suspend the Treasury's commitment to convert dollars into gold. Preventing a run on gold was not, as some asserted at the time, the major reason for these measures, although it was a precipitating factor. The President's main goal was to boost domestic employment. Improving the U.S. trade balance was one important way of doing so. Other steps taken at Camp David to increase employment included creating incentives for domestic investment and repealing the excise tax on autos. Nixon also took a range of measures to arrest inflation, such as a 90-day period of wage and price controls and a cut in government spending.

In the period that followed these measures (which came to be known in Japan as the Nixon shock), the United States set about to convince other nations to revalue their currencies and to reduce restrictions impeding market access for U.S. exports. Having been frustrated by the unwillingness of a number of countries, such as Japan and France, to change their parities before August, and by America's inability to obtain trade concessions abroad, the Administration now felt that it had more leverage as the result of the President's actions. Its goal was to improve the U.S. trade balance in the next year, 1972, from a projected $4 billion deficit to a surplus of $9 billion. Exchange rate realignment, as opposed to reform of the monetary system (then seen by the President as a longer-term and somewhat academic exercise), was key to achieving that surplus.

Nixon's actions set in motion an intensive negotiating process. The Europeans felt that the desired $13 billion swing in the U.S. trade balance implied too much of a deterioration in their own trade positions. And they wanted the United States to "contribute" to the exchange rate realignment by devaluing the dollar vis-à-vis gold. France, in particular, sought this U.S. contribution because its government did not want to revalue the franc vis-à-vis gold, reducing the number of francs an ounce of gold would fetch. French officials feared that they would then be vulnerable to the domestic accusation that they had lowered the value (in terms of francs) of the considerable amounts of gold that French citizens customarily store in their homes and backyards.

The Europeans also insisted that the United States promptly restore convertibility of the dollar into gold. They reasoned that

Don Wright, *The Miami News*, 1971

"More gum, Connally—and get a longer stick"

the United States, subject again to the discipline of the convertibility requirement, might then lose gold from its reserves and be forced to devalue the dollar by economic circumstances rather than by agreement. And the Europeans wanted the United States to lift the newly imposed surcharge on imports in order to restore pre-August access of European goods to the U.S. market.

The United States resisted devaluation of the dollar. In announcing his August 15 measures, the President had emphasized that "we must protect the position of the American dollar as a pillar of monetary stability in the world." He was told by domestic political advisers that breaking the sacrosanct 35:1 dollar-gold relationship would be portrayed as a sign of U.S. weakness. Concerns were also expressed that a devaluation would make the dollar suspect in the future and thus less attractive as a reserve asset. And there were fears of a possible run-up in the price of gold on the private market in anticipation of further declines in the dollar. Moreover, some argued the very mention of a possible dollar devaluation might prompt foreign governments or private dollar holders (both of whose dollar assets had expanded at a dramatic rate) to sell at least a part of their holdings, which would cause the currency's value to drop precipitously.

As time passed, it became clear to Washington that some U.S. "contribution" to a currency realignment was necessary. From an economic perspective it mattered little whether others appreciated their currencies or the United States devalued its currency so long as the magnitude of the realignment was adequate.

Aftermath of the Shock

Internationally, the Nixon-Connally shock had drawn attention to the need for a better alignment of currencies. It had, parenthetically, also helped launch a new round of multilateral trade negotiations under the General Agreement on Tariffs and Trade (GATT). In these respects the shock had the intended effect. The next problem was how to use the new U.S. leverage to obtain a currency realignment of the magnitude sought by the United States.

During this period, Federal Reserve Chairman Arthur F. Burns, this author (who was then senior economic adviser to national security adviser Henry A. Kissinger) and other members of the National Security Council staff regularly compared notes on the reports received from U.S. embassies and other sources abroad. Most of these reports indicated that the shock had forced other governments to acknowledge the need for a currency realignment. However, the reports also noted that prolonged maintenance of the U.S. surcharge on imports could lead foreign governments to try to boost their own leverage by not implementing the last stages of the previous round of tariff reductions (the Kennedy Round).

At this point, neither Burns nor Kissinger felt prepared to suggest a sharp reversal of the U.S. position, or to take on Connally directly. Nor would it have been wise from an international negotiating point of view to pull back too quickly. The substantial realignment of currencies the United States was calling for was indeed necessary; an agreement which fell short of that would only lead to another crisis at some future date. Burns and the author, on behalf of Kissinger, did agree, however, to send

26

the President separate memoranda on the growing risks of a prolonged international economic impasse. The U.S. import surcharge, both memoranda concluded, would become a wasting asset if other governments imposed import barriers of their own or if it caused them to become more inflexible in monetary or other economic negotiations. Kissinger also feared that any recession in Western Europe and Japan attributable to U.S. actions would cause a major rift in U.S. alliances and a weakening in the stability of countries important to U.S. foreign policy and security.

In November 1971, Nixon recognized that the time had come to seek a solution and conveyed this view to Connally. There was still, of course, the issue of how to bring about a satisfactory currency realignment. One proposal coming from within the Administration was to try to isolate the French from the rest of the European Economic Community (EEC, or Common Market) and seek an accommodation with West Germany. (France at the time was the European nation most insistent that the dollar be devalued vis-à-vis gold.) West Germany, some argued, could be convinced to revalue the deutsche mark and press other European countries to revalue their currencies, although by a smaller amount. These combined revaluations would relieve the United States of the need to devalue the dollar. If West Germany could lead Western Europe in this direction, so the logic went, it would be a political victory for the President and a face-saving solution for the United States because the 35:1 dollar-gold relationship would remain intact.

The other approach was to try to reach an agreement with France on a combination of a U.S. devaluation vis-à-vis gold and a lesser devaluation or a standstill for the franc vis-à-vis gold; other currencies, chiefly the yen and deutsche mark, would be substantially revalued. Such a procedure would achieve the U.S. competitive objective, relieve France of the need to revalue vis-à-vis gold, and pave the way for compromise with West Germany and the rest of the EEC.

Many on the staff of the NSC (including this author) and Federal Reserve Board argued that the first approach, isolating

UPI/Bettmann Newsphotos

Presidents Richard M. Nixon and Georges Pompidou during their December 1971 meeting in the Azores on dollar devaluation

France, would exacerbate divisions in the EEC. In any case, the West German government would probably have been unwilling to reach an accommodation with the United States at the expense of its relations with France, which would have provoked a major crisis in the Common Market.

Azores Meeting

Nixon agreed to take the second alternative. President Pompidou was subsequently approached and a meeting with Nixon was arranged for mid-December 1971 in the Azores.

Nixon's trip to the Azores was in large measure prepared by the skillful negotiating tactics of Connally and Paul Volcker, then Connally's under secretary for monetary affairs, at a meeting of the Ministers of the Group of Ten in Rome from November 29 to December 1, 1971. Prior to that, Western Europe had pressed the United States hard to make a contribution to a currency realignment by devaluing the dollar. At the Rome meeting,

Volcker stunned the others. He not only indicated a willingness to devalue the dollar but also went well beyond foreign expectations by suggesting a devaluation of 10 or 15 percent! This, other countries feared, would leave them at a major competitive disadvantage vis-à-vis the United States. After the Volcker suggestion at Rome, negotiations concentrated not on whether but on how much the United States would devalue and on how much other countries would allow their currencies to appreciate vis-à-vis the soon-to-be-lowered dollar.

In the Azores, on December 13 and 14, Nixon and Pompidou, with Kissinger doing a major share of the negotiating with Pompidou, agreed on the magnitude of the dollar's devaluation—from the prevailing $35 to a new $38 per ounce of gold. The yen and deutsche mark were to be revalued by a percentage to be negotiated later.

Smithsonian Agreement

A broader and more detailed agreement on realignment among the other Group of Ten currencies was reached later in December at the Smithsonian Institution in Washington. The dollar, the United States confirmed, was to be devalued as earlier agreed by Nixon and Pompidou. The French franc would retain its existing gold parity. There were to be sizable increases in the exchange value of the yen, deutsche mark and Swiss franc and small increases for a few other currencies. The net result was a weighted dollar decline of about 10 percent against the other Group of Ten currencies. Currencies were to be allowed to fluctuate in a band of 2.25 percent above and below their new parities, compared to 1 percent before. The estimated improvement in the U.S. trade balance was scaled down considerably, from the original U.S. goal of $13 billion to less than $10 billion.

The Smithsonian meeting marked the first collective agreement on a realignment of world currencies. What caused the old system of currency alignments to fail, concluded Robert Solomon, for many years the senior international economist at the Federal Reserve Board, "was the failure of the adjustment process." Had other nations, such as Japan and the surplus countries of Europe, "been readier to adjust their exchange rates upward as the U.S. trade surplus eroded in the second half of the 1960s, the system might have been preserved and it would not have been necessary for the United States to suspend convertibility in August 1971."

President Nixon advertised the Smithsonian Agreement as the "most significant monetary agreement in the history of the world." It soon proved to be something less. New pressures began appearing within months of the Smithsonian meeting.

The EEC took a new step in mid-1972 to try to stabilize member nations' currencies vis-à-vis one another. It established what was informally known as the snake—a band within which EEC currencies could fluctuate in relation to each other. That band was 1.125 percent on either side of the "central" rate. Since the EEC's limits were half of the recently expanded IMF zone (nicknamed the tunnel) of 2.25 percent on either side of the central rate, the EEC band was dubbed the snake in the tunnel. The snake was the forerunner of the current European Monetary System.

The Dam Breaks in 1973

Early in 1973 exchange rate volatility increased. During the first week in February, West Germany had to buy billions of dollars to limit the deutsche mark's appreciation. The enormous amount of deutsche marks sold by the German Bundesbank to purchase dollars created an unwelcome potential for inflation in West Germany. Belgium and the Netherlands had to undertake similarly painful interventions. During the same period, Japan had to purchase large sums of dollars to keep the yen from piercing the top of the tunnel. Saturated with dollars, it eventually ceased its currency intervention activities—in effect permitting the yen to float upward without hindrance. In the face of large capital inflows, primarily from Italy, the Swiss franc also floated. So then did Italy's lira.

This time the chaos was too great to permit a negotiated solution. The United States was suffering from a major capital outflow and a still-disappointing trade performance. There was no chance for a formal meeting to realign currencies. On February 12, after a round-the-world trip by Volcker to inform other nations of its intentions, the United States devalued the dollar by 10 percent vis-à-vis gold.

This bold move, however, did not stem the tide. Speculation against the dollar continued. The West Germans and others were forced to absorb billions of dollars more to prevent a further decline in the dollar and a sharp new appreciation of their own currencies. The United States did little intervention on its own—a source of considerable dismay to the Europeans.

In March it became hopeless to defend existing exchange rates. Futilely, the major industrialized nations sought to calm the exchange markets. A meeting of the United States, the EEC countries, Japan and other industrialized nations issued a communiqué asserting that "existing relationships between parities and central rates, following the recent realignment, corre-

"I didn't even understand the old system!"

spond. . .to the economic requirements and. . .these relationships will make an effective monetary contribution to a better balance of international payments."

Their efforts to quiet the market were to no avail. Market pressures persisted. In mid-March six members of the EEC decided to float the snake vis-à-vis other currencies (Britain, Ireland and Italy were floating independently). Under the terms of the "joint float," the six would keep their own currencies aligned but would no longer intervene to maintain a preset relationship with the dollar. In time the United States also decided to float its currency.

4

Floating Rates

The decision to float currencies in early 1973 enabled governments to extricate themselves from a major and seemingly
uncontrollable international currency crisis. No new set of
exchange rate parities appeared to have credibility in the market.
Floating exchange rates were widely accepted as a necessity at the
time. They were equally widely viewed as temporary—a means
of finding "market-oriented" parities or some form of central
rates while talks on monetary reform progressed.

The forum that emerged late in 1972 to consider changes in the
monetary system was not, as previously, the Group of Ten but a
new Committee of Twenty (constituted as the Committee on
Reform of the International Monetary System and Related
Issues). The expanded group was very much the brainchild of
John Connally, who sought to dilute what he felt was the
excessive European representation in the Group of Ten by adding
a number of developing countries to the discussions. It also served
to underscore that a number of developing countries were indeed
now playing a greater role in the world economy and merited
seats at the table.

While the preoccupation of negotiations in the 1960s was

liquidity, resulting in the creation of the useful if underutilized Special Drawing Rights, the monetary reform debate of the 1970s centered on the adjustment process—the changes in economic policies or in exchange rates needed to reduce a country's balance-of-payments surplus or deficit. Adjustment and liquidity are, to be sure, closely linked. Countries with a great deal of liquidity, that is, ample reserves of gold or currency, or with the ability to borrow large sums to bolster their reserves, can finance large deficits for a long time and therefore avoid or delay policy or exchange rate adjustments to reduce their balance-of-payments deficits. Countries with little liquidity must devalue their currencies or otherwise adjust very quickly by tightening domestic demand to curtail imports. In the past, countries faced with the need to make trade-offs between financing current account deficits and adjusting to eliminate them had too often tended to choose the former. This made adjustment all the more painful when it ultimately had to be effected. The experience of the late 1960s and the early 1970s heightened recognition that if adjustment did not take place in a timely fashion, even a country with a large liquid reserve pool would quickly run out of money.

The difficult and contentious issue facing the Committee of Twenty centered on the question of who would adjust, when, and by how much. Perceptions among nations differed considerably on these issues. The United States felt strongly that countries with large balance-of-payments surpluses should, as a matter of course, revalue their currencies and thus help deficit countries to reduce their imbalances. It complained that the Bretton Woods system had no incentives, or penalties, to encourage or force surplus countries to revalue their currencies. The United States argued that, unlike countries which lose their reserves when they suffer from prolonged deficits and thus must devalue their currencies, surplus countries have no pressures imposed on them. This contention was not completely accurate. The events of 1973 demonstrated that if a country such as West Germany is compelled to absorb large amounts of foreign currency to prevent an appreciation of its own currency, it will ultimately suffer an increase in its domestic money supply and the consequent threat of inflation. Under these circumstances, it will feel pressure to revalue. However, there were few examples of this occurring. The U.S. argument was largely valid.

The Futile Search for Symmetry

The United States sought symmetry in the system to ensure that there were incentives and penalties for both surplus and deficit nations. In response to the American position, Western Europe cited the familiar argument that the United States enjoyed a major advantage by virtue of the willingness of other countries to hold large amounts of dollars in their reserves. Western Europe awaited a return to dollar-gold convertibility, and meanwhile sought to force the United States to "settle" foreign holdings of dollars in assets—gold or other foreign currencies—rather than have other nations indefinitely finance U.S. deficits by increasing their holdings of dollars.

The United States withheld a commitment to "asset settlement" pending agreement on symmetrical adjustment. Western Europe (with occasional, albeit low-key, support from Japan) sought agreement on convertibility before acquiescing in rules for symmetry. It contended that with convertibility there would be less need for symmetry because the United States would not get into large payments deficits.

To bridge the differences, the United States proposed a system of graduated pressures based on a "reserve indicator." If a country's reserves increased above a given level, that would be taken as a sign that the country should adjust by revaluing its exchange rate or modifying its domestic policy—for example, by increasing domestic demand through budgetary stimulus. Such an action would reduce that nation's current account surplus and the inflow of foreign currency into its reserves. Moreover, if a country's reserves exceeded the indicator, that country would lose the right to convert into gold or other currencies its holdings of reserves in excess of the indicator.

Under this same scheme, if total reserves were to fall below a certain level, that would signal the need for a country to devalue its currency or to take other measures, such as tighter domestic fiscal policies, to cure its deficit and stem the decline in its reserves.

Western Europe resisted this set of proposals. First, it opposed the idea that the sanction of nonconvertibility would automatically go into effect when the reserve indicator was reached by a nation in surplus. This objection led the United States ultimately to make the indicator "presumptive," so that a large surplus situation would trigger a discussion among the nations involved to determine whether there were extenuating circumstances that merited an "override" of the indicator. Europeans also believed that as reserves moved toward the upside or downside indicator levels, speculators would anticipate changes in exchange rates. Such anticipation, they felt, would start destabilizing capital flows. In response, U.S. officials, and particularly Paul Volcker, stressed the need for objective criteria—a reserve indicator would be one—to exert *discipline* over national policies. If the rules permitted too much flexibility, there would be no discipline. Absent hard and fast rules, a nation's leaders could not point to external reasons to justify exchange rate changes or tough domestic measures needed to correct the country's international imbalance.

An effort was made to reconcile the differences among the parties in 1973. At Reykjavik, Iceland, while President Nixon was closeted with President Pompidou, Secretary of the Treasury George P. Shultz, French Finance Minister Valéry Giscard d'Estaing, Volcker, Giscard's deputy Claude Pierre-Brossollet and this author, as Kissinger's economic adviser, participated in an adjoining room in a four-hour review of monetary issues and positions. Giscard again emphasized the importance the French attached to mandatory convertibility of dollars into gold by the United States. Shultz reemphasized the need for symmetry and argued in favor of the reserve indicator proposal, including denial of convertibility for reserves above the indicator. France subsequently sought to promote a compromise, but no agreement was reached.

As further efforts were made to narrow U.S.-European differences, the oil crisis intervened. Turmoil in currency markets

Leaders attending the Rambouillet economic summit: (l. to r.) Takeo Miki (Japan), Aldo Moro (Italy) Harold Wilson (Britain), Gerald Ford (U.S.), Valerie Giscard d'Estaing (France) and Helmut Schmidt (West Germany)

resulted from the sharp price increase in oil and the expectation that these increases would spread to other commodities and services. Therefore virtually all observers, including those who in principle favored fixed rates, reconciled themselves to the indefinite continuation of floating currencies.

Rambouillet and Jamaica

In November 1975, after months of negotiations between U.S. and French financial officials, the first economic summit of Western leaders—at Rambouillet, France—officially recognized the temporary inevitability of floating exchange rates. But the leaders also pledged that their "monetary authorities will act to counter disorderly market conditions, or erratic fluctuations, in exchange rates." That is, the floating was not to be entirely free, as advocated by its academic and other proponents. This author, who served as an American "sherpa" (planner) for the summit and the note-taker in President Gerald R. Ford's discussions with the other heads of state, recalls that however artful the agreed language was, it masked a major difference in philosophy between, chiefly, the United States and France. The United States, at the time, was becoming more and more enchanted with the notion of a long period of floating rates to release it from what its officials, particularly Secretary of the Treasury William Simon, Shultz's successor, regarded as the shackles and rigidities of fixed rates. The French sought a return to the discipline of fixed rates and convertibility of the U.S. dollar.

The agreement reached among the Western leaders at Rambouillet contained something for both France and the United States. It recognized the need for the French government to be able to tell its citizens that it had not given up the goal of returning to fixed rates. And France obtained a U.S. commitment to try to stabilize exchange rates. The United States achieved agreement on its goal of maintaining considerable flexibility in the monetary system and avoided a commitment to return prematurely to a fixed-rate system or convertibility.

The Rambouillet accord formed the basis of a subsequent agreement on the Second Amendment of the Articles of Agreement of the IMF, reached in Jamaica in 1976 among members of the IMF Interim Committee. In early 1974 the Interim Committee had replaced the Committee of Twenty; members of the latter had concluded that they could not agree on monetary reform in the tumultuous circumstances then prevailing. The Jamaica agreement serves to this day as the framework for the floating rate system.

The IMF Second Amendment codifies a number of points. Governments pledge to foster orderly underlying economic and financial conditions, avoid erratic movements in exchange rates and refrain from manipulating exchange rates to either prevent balance-of-payments adjustment or gain an unfair advantage over other nations. The IMF is given responsibility for exercising "firm surveillance" over the exchange rate policies of members. A country is permitted to choose among a variety of exchange rate regimes: floating, tying to the currency of another nation whose exchange rate is floating, maintaining an exchange rate tied to several currencies, or fixing vis-à-vis SDRs. (Fixing to gold was not permitted.) To leave the door open to further monetary reform, the Fund was permitted, by an 85 percent majority, to "make provision for general exchange rate arrangements." The 85 percent figure was inserted by the United States. It has more than 15 percent of the vote in the IMF, hence the United States could block any return to a fixed rate system that it felt contained inadequate provisions for symmetrical adjustment. The amendment also enhanced the role of the SDR by making it easier for governments to transfer and use SDRs, abolished the official price of gold and returned some gold held by the IMF to Fund members. (An additional amount was sold for the benefit of poorer nations.)

The flexibility built into the Second Amendment, which permitted each nation to choose its own exchange rate regime, led to a mixed bag of currency arrangements. Few countries actually chose to float freely. Most decided to link their currencies to the dollar in some way, to the weighted average of a "basket" of major currencies, or collectively to one another in the European snake. Among the major currencies, the U.S. dollar, the British pound, the yen, the Canadian dollar and the Australian dollar were allowed to float more or less freely.

Floating Wins Support

It should be noted that between 1973, when generalized floating began, and 1976, the notion of a more enduring float had gained support—particularly in the United States Treasury. Secretary Simon constantly underscored the importance he attached to allowing the market to determine the appropriate exchange rate for each currency. His arguments received strong support in the U.S. academic and business communities. Proponents of a system of floating rates argued that this would enable countries to pursue independent domestic policies because balance-of-payments surpluses or deficits, which resulted from differences in domestic policies, would be reflected in movements in exchange rates. They in turn would reduce the payments imbalances that might result. A country with a current account deficit would expect to see its currency depreciate; one with a surplus would expect to see its currency appreciate. As a result both types of imbalances would ultimately be eliminated.

Exchange rates, supporters of the float argued, would no longer be the parameters for domestic policy, as they were under the fixed rate regime. In that regime, domestic policy was to be conducted so as to maintain preset exchange rates. Under the floating exchange rate system, exchange rates were to be a vehicle for reducing payments imbalances that resulted from differing domestic policies.

In reality, however, floating rates have been so heavily buffeted by large international flows of capital that they have all-too-frequently failed to induce timely balance-of-payments adjustments. As a result, rather than serving an equilibrating function, floating rates often have led to major distortions in trade. Robert V. Roosa, former under secretary of the treasury for monetary affairs, put the matter as follows: "Under the fixed rate system capital flows were expected to play a subsidiary role, tending to reinforce an already impending exchange rate adjustment brought about by comparative price changes and shifts in trade. But under conditions of floating, capital flows have more and more become the prime determinants of exchange rates, thereby imposing on the current account the burden not only of adjusting for changes in relative prices or trading potentials but also of overcompensating for excesses induced by capital flows."

Instability in world currency markets prompted Western Europe to consolidate and institutionalize the snake. The snake became a bit ragged during the 1970s as several participants peeled off and floated independently. In 1979, a new attempt was made to put European currency relationships in order. According to one of the European Monetary System's godfathers, Robert Triffin, now emeritus professor of economics at Yale, the EMS had two objectives: "in the short run, the desire to make the national economies of the member countries of the European Community less dependent on the vagaries of an unstable paper dollar," and "in the longer run, the desire to progress toward a full economic, monetary, and therefore political union of the Community."

Under the new EMS, the member currencies would be maintained within a zone of plus or minus 2.25 percent of one another. It also was agreed that corrective policy actions would be taken if any one currency diverged too greatly from another. To help countries to intervene in currency markets in order to keep exchange rates within the band, the European Monetary Cooperation Fund (known by its French acronym FECOM) was established; it was supplied with contributions of gold and dollars from members' reserves. Western Europe also established the European Currency Unit (ECU), whose value was based on the weighted average of currencies of member countries.

The EMS has demonstrated considerable success in moderating exchange rate movements among its participating currencies, especially when compared to the enormous volatility that other exchange rates have exhibited (see Chapter 6). The EMS has done so chiefly by providing a framework for better coordination of domestic economic policies, a key goal of which was reducing inflation, and by establishing the practice of coordinated exchange rate intervention. When neither has succeeded in maintaining a currency within the EMS band limits, currencies have been realigned. The ECU has evolved into an important instrument in world capital markets; billions of dollars worth of Eurobonds are now denominated in ECUs.

5

The Oil Crisis, the Debt Crisis and IMF Conditionality

The 1973–74 oil crisis, and the major payments imbalances which it brought about, put enormous pressure on the international monetary system. In particular, it highlighted the difficulties of deciding on the proper trade-off between correcting economic policies in order to reduce current account deficits and financing those deficits by borrowing from abroad or drawing down reserves.

One of the key roles of the IMF throughout its history has been to provide temporary or short-term financing to countries suffering from payments imbalances. A country's access to the first, or reserve, *tranche* (the French word for slice), previously called the gold tranche, is automatic. This is the case because the country using this tranche is merely borrowing currencies up to an amount equivalent to the value of the gold or foreign currencies it had deposited in the Fund earlier. This tranche amounts to 25 percent of a country's overall IMF quota (its total borrowing allowance). Access to the next 25 percent (the first "credit tranche") is relatively easy. To draw further on the Fund, the country must demonstrate that its domestic policies are aimed at reestablishing balance-of-payments equilibrium. Fund "conditionality," the policy changes that the IMF asks a country to make before it approves drawings beyond the first credit tranche, generally involves a range of measures to curtail borrowing and boost exports. These include reducing inflation, increasing taxes, cutting government spending and slashing subsidies. In many cases the Fund and a member country will agree on a program of policy improvements without an immediate drawing on Fund resources. The country has the future right to draw resources up to and in some cases beyond its total quota in the Fund, if necessary, as long as it remains in compliance with its agreement with the Fund. Between 1952 and 1970 the IMF approved well over 200 such "standby agreements."

In the first stages of the oil crisis, demands on the IMF increased substantially. The Fund responded by developing new types of lending programs, with modified standards of conditionality, in order to accommodate the situation. These included: first, an "oil facility" (a special line of credit with rather low conditionality) to assist countries adversely affected by the rise in oil prices, provided they took measures to reduce their payments deficits; second, a trust fund which provided still easier standards of conditionality for loans to very poor countries affected by the crisis. These loans were financed by sales of some of the IMF's gold. Both programs have now been discontinued.

The Fund Extends Itself

A more enduring change in IMF practices was the creation of the Extended Fund Facility. Inaugurated in 1974, the facility was designed to provide medium-term financial assistance to countries that have a "serious payments imbalance relating to structural maladjustments in production and trade," or in which "slow growth and an inherently weak balance of payments" prevent an effective development policy. Total borrowing from the Extended Fund Facility could be substantially above a country's normal quota, and the borrower could take a longer time to pay back the money than under a normal Fund standby agreement.

The Extended Fund Facility in many ways substantially

changed the Fund from a short-term oriented, relatively passive institution to one with longer-term objectives, quarterly targets to insure that policies are on course and an active role in encouraging and monitoring national policies. Adolfo C. Diz, former president of the Central Bank of Argentina, described the importance of the change as follows: "The idea of combining medium-term objectives and policies with a more detailed short-term set of specific policies and measures . . . will probably have a highly positive effect on the task of persons responsible for economic management in developing countries." The IMF, in other words, was now directly involved in domestic policymaking, and had become a force that government officials seeking internal policy changes could evoke to support their own positions. Often the presence of such an outside force can tip the balance in favor of a particular policy and permit a country's leaders to shift to the IMF some of the "political heat" for painful domestic measures—heat that might otherwise be directed at the leaders themselves.

The Fund also created the Supplementary Financing Facility at the end of the 1970s. Under that facility the Fund borrowed from oil-exporting countries and others in relatively strong payments positions to increase its lending to countries with payments problems.

New practices and facilities enabled the IMF to play a significant role in the oil crisis and in the debt crisis that followed. During much of the 1970s countries experiencing deep payments imbalances drew heavily on the IMF. Annual average drawings by its members, especially following the oil crisis of 1973-74, roughly tripled from the levels of the 1960s. The second oil shock, following the Iranian revolution of 1979, led to a series of new requests for IMF funds.

Although the IMF played an important role in helping countries to withstand the full blow of the oil crisis, the bulk of new funding for the larger developing countries came from the private sectors of other nations. Private bank lending was increased in the mid-1970s to cushion the first oil shock, and then in the early 1980s to cushion the second. Many developing countries were able to borrow from Western banks, often at relatively attractive interest rates. Absent such financing they would have had to cut back on imports other than oil and curtail domestic demand. Instead they borrowed to pay their higher oil import bills and to finance the high level of imports of other products needed to satisfy and support their rapid domestic growth. The ability of oil-importing countries to finance large trade deficits enabled many of them to avoid politically unpopular belt-tightening measures. Borrowing from banks also enabled these nations to avoid difficult structural reforms: selling state enterprises to the private sector; closing or modernizing inefficient factories; eliminating costly subsidies.

After the second oil shock the industrialized governments decided to launch a major attack on inflation. Most of Western Europe and Japan did so by reducing government budget deficits; the United States relied heavily on tighter monetary policy, while allowing its budget deficits to increase. The net result of such policies was sharply higher interest rates around the world and a dramatic slowdown in world economic growth. Because of higher interest rates, the debt-servicing costs on new loans became very high. Interest rates on older loans that were rolled over also increased.

The large appreciation of the dollar from 1980 until early 1985 imposed another cost. It particularly hit developing countries that received a large portion of their foreign earnings in weakening currencies but, having borrowed heavily in dollars, had to service most of their debts in the strengthening dollar. In addition, slow foreign demand, resulting from tough anti-inflation policies in major industrialized nations, served to retard the growth of exports from debtor countries, thereby lowering their ability to earn the foreign exchange necessary to service their debts.

And Now the Debt Crisis

The oil crisis, high interest rates, poor domestic policies in many developing countries, and the economic slowdown in the world set the stage for the debt crisis of the 1980s. Through much of the 1970s and until mid-1982, it was the general view of most developing countries that their balance-of-payments deficits could be sustained for a long time. Hence, they could be financed by new borrowing rather than reduced by adoption of tough domestic economic policies. Such policies would have cut demand for imports, thus limiting the need for external financing and enabling existing debt to be serviced more easily.

Many developing nations, particularly in Latin America, preferred to borrow rather than take strong domestic measures of this type. And having easy access for a time to bank credit, many could avoid borrowing from the IMF and thus not have to implement the types of policy improvements the Fund would require as conditions for providing funds—improvements which might have averted the worst aspects of the debt crisis.

Borrowers and the banks both underestimated the extent to which interest rates would rise in real (inflation-adjusted) terms and growth in industrialized-country markets would weaken. The result of the kinds and amounts of borrowing done under conditions prior to 1982 was the multibillion dollar debt problem that has disrupted growth in much of Latin America and other parts of the Third World.

Standby Agreements

It is worth noting that, compared with Latin America, countries such as South Korea and Turkey, which made painful policy adjustments early in the 1980s, India and China, which avoided overborrowing, and many Southeast Asian nations, which avoided massive government subsidies and economic distortions arising from currency misalignments, have been able to cope with economic difficulties emanating from outside perturbations with relatively little disruption to their domestic economies.

The IMF, with strong support from the U.S. Treasury and the Federal Reserve Board, played the pivotal role in developing and implementing a strategy to address the debt problem for those countries that did get into trouble. It worked with commercial banks, the governments of industrialized countries and debtor governments to construct emergency rescue packages for countries such as Mexico, Brazil and Argentina. The key component in all these packages was an IMF standby agreement. As part of such agreements the Fund and individual governments would negotiate adjustment programs, with specific targets that the Fund would monitor. Such programs would typically involve a cut in government expenditures, a currency devaluation, a tighter monetary policy and a reduction in government subsidies. The programs were intended to pave the way for the debtor country to receive money from the IMF, reschedule loans with creditor banks and obtain new bank loans.

These standby agreements did not achieve the type of results the Fund expected on the basis of its earlier experience. Many Third World governments were remarkably successful in reducing their large trade deficits, and some, like Brazil, soon produced an enormous trade surplus. But for most debtor countries, internal adjustment proved more difficult than external adjustment. Subsidies continued to make heavy demands on government financial resources. Many governments were reluctant to reduce the number of workers in state enterprises and cut wages. The private sector in many parts of Latin America found it difficult to repay old debts and to obtain new financing.

Over a period of time IMF programs came to be associated in the public mind with austerity. Although it is true that debtor countries with IMF standby agreements had to endure a substantial measure of austerity, that was largely the result of their having run out of credit. A country that can no longer obtain financing for a current account deficit must inevitably do some belt-tightening to reduce that deficit. Although Fund programs may have encouraged exaggerated expectations and distributed the costs of domestic adjustment in controversial—that is, socially unequal—ways, the requirement for adjustment and a period of lower growth was an unavoidable result of overborrowing during earlier periods. Indeed many developing countries would probably have suffered far more had the Fund not become involved. Without IMF resources and without new commercial bank lending contingent on the country having an IMF-sanctioned program (see below), the eventual adjustments and austerity required would have been even more painful.

Larosière at the Helm

The Fund's prominence during this period was by no means foreordained. It was in large measure the result of the leadership of its managing director, Jacques de Larosière. He put the IMF into the pivotal position in the international effort to address the debt problem. He did so by two major means. First, he elevated the Fund's standby program to the status of a seal of approval for a country's domestic economic policy. As a result, commercial banks withheld new loans, or the rescheduling of old ones, until a standby agreement was reached between the debtor country and the Fund. This added considerably to the Fund's leverage over the country in question. Second, he strengthened the IMF's influence with commercial banks. The Fund pressed these banks to extend new financing to and reschedule loan repayments from countries that had agreed to standby arrangements. Because the banks could not themselves easily negotiate policy reforms with debtor countries, they welcomed the leadership of the IMF in doing so and supplied additional funds to support the IMF's role. They also welcomed the large amounts of Fund resources that accompanied the agreement of a high-debt developing country to a program the Fund found acceptable.

The IMF's efforts to help solve the debt problem moved it closer to the role of the World Bank. The World Bank, as discussed earlier, has played a key role in supporting development in the Third World. Almost all its money comes from two sources: direct contributions by governments to its "soft loan" window, the International Development Association (IDA), for lending to the world's poorer countries; and from borrowing in world capital markets. To support the latter, member governments provide small monetary contributions (known as "paid-in-capital") plus much larger amounts of "callable capital"; these constitute the resources for its "ordinary" lending to less poor but still needy developing nations. The callable capital in effect serves as collateral for World Bank borrowing.

Before the debt crisis, the World Bank concentrated on financing specific *projects* in developing nations. These projects—dams, highways, rural electrification—were key to building the infrastructure and productive capacity of recipient countries. But as slow economic growth in the world led to overcapacity in many sectors of many economies, the number of economically viable new projects for the World Bank to finance was reduced. And since debtor countries in any case required funds that could be disbursed quickly and in substantial amounts, the World Bank began to provide more adjustment loans to help *sectors* of the economy such as agriculture become more efficient. Many of these loans, known as policy-based loans, were in practice similar to the balance-of-payments lending that was normally the responsibility of the IMF.

Thus, the World Bank was moving from project loans to sectoral loans aimed at structural reform, while the IMF was also beginning to concern itself with improving policies in important sectors—such as reducing domestic subsidies for agriculture or power generation, or curbing the use of excessive labor in, say, steel production. The World Bank was also becoming more involved with the overall economic policies of developing countries: even the best of projects would fail to live up to expectations if such policies were inappropriate. This convergence of functions called for greater interaction between the World Bank and the Fund. Ideally both should be encouraging the same types of policy improvements and seeing that their loans to any given country are mutually supportive. Such coordination has not been smooth, since each institution prides itself on a certain amount of autonomy and is accustomed to taking different approaches to problems. It has taken considerable time to integrate the expertise of both organizations in developing a unified strategy for individual countries.

Baker Takes a Hand

The U.S. government sought to get the World Bank more involved in resolving the debt problem. At the 1985 annual meeting of the World Bank and IMF in Seoul, South Korea, Secretary of the Treasury James A. Baker 3d stressed the importance of resolving the Third World debt problem by boosting national economic growth rather than by more domestic austerity. Such a policy would require the debtor countries to pursue market-oriented growth policies, the commercial banks to provide more funds, and the World Bank to disburse loans more rapidly. The U.S. goal was to increase the flow of financial resources to countries making sufficient progress in improving their policies.

Although Secretary Baker's initiative encouraged the IMF to maintain a central role in dealing with the debt problem, it also recognized that the Fund required some help from the World Bank. The Fund's role over time had come under greater criticism in the Third World due to the slow growth in many of those nations maintaining IMF programs. In early 1986, the Fund's leverage was further weakened as the commercial banks, for the first time since the beginning of the debt crisis, agreed to a rescheduling agreement in the absence of a standby agreement with the IMF, with Brazil.

Brazil, the largest Third World debtor, had vastly improved its trade performance by 1986. However, its internal performance, measured by its high rate of inflation and large government borrowing from domestic sources, did not meet IMF targets. Despite these shortfalls, many banks felt that Brazil's improvements on the external side were sufficient to merit new funds. The point, however, is that the link between an IMF program and bank rescheduling was broken. This break will tend to reduce IMF leverage. It may also have adverse consequences for banks, because the major negotiator of conditionality, the IMF, will now be unable to claim that banks will not lend in the absence of a standby program. In short, the IMF's job has become more difficult.

Does this mean that the IMF's role in fashioning debt remedies is declining? The answer is unclear. On the one hand the commercial banks cannot themselves negotiate the same conditionality as the Fund. Thus the Fund will continue to be important to the banks. Likewise, debtor countries will from time to time want new resources from the IMF; and they will want to get its seal of approval to attract new private-sector loans.

On the other hand, if commercial banks, for their own valid

reasons, reschedule or provide new loans to debtor countries that are either out of compliance with the Fund, or have not made standby agreements, the IMF's leverage in negotiating conditionality could be reduced. The IMF could also find itself less credible in suggesting to a debtor country that commercial banks will not lend to it unless it implements a domestic program agreed to by the Fund.

Moreover, the Fund's difficulties in fashioning successful policies for a number of debtor countries have somewhat reduced international confidence in IMF prescriptions and in its ability to persuade debtor countries to adhere to them. To be sure, the major reason for the resistance of debtor countries to such prescriptions is often political, and the IMF cannot fairly be blamed for that. Nor can Fund programs work well when the world economy is very weak; the increase in Third World exports, which IMF agreements typically envisage, cannot take place while developed nations experience feeble growth or raise barriers against goods from the Third World.

Whatever the reason, difficulties in encouraging successful adjustment have somewhat diminished the IMF's influence in dealing with debtor nations. The Fund is, nonetheless, still very much at the center of the process, and its continued leadership is an indispensable part of any meaningful world response to the debt problem. As Secretary Baker's speech in Seoul suggested, no country and no group of commercial banks can solve this problem without the IMF.

What the IMF Can Do

This is not to say that the approach of the IMF to the debt problem cannot or should not change. Indeed, in the future the Fund's role in the world economy is likely to be modified in a number of ways. In recent years the IMF, in large measure through standby agreements and the Extended Fund Facility, has been more active than before in suggesting policy changes to countries facing balance-of-payments difficulties. It is now in a position to go one step further and exercise active surveillance by providing advice to countries that appear to be heading for debt trouble before they need to ask the IMF for financial help. It can also work out better tailored performance targets for use in monitoring the progress of countries that have payments problems. And the IMF might encourage larger numbers of countries to seek its advice and technical support for domestic policy reforms even if they do not need a standby agreement. Frequently advice and support by the IMF can enable a country to obtain commercial bank funds without having to call on Fund resources.

A Brief Review

A review of the IMF's role in managing balance-of-payments problems resulting from the oil shocks and the debt crisis suggests several points.

First, the Fund was instrumental in the shift from an emphasis on financing deficits to a stress on encouraging and supporting policy adjustments needed to reduce such deficits.

Second, the Fund demonstrated a remarkable flexibility in moving beyond its traditional, and relatively passive, role to the activist role of galvanizing international support for emergency financial rescue packages.

Third, over this period an IMF seal of approval for a country's economic policy came to play a decisive role in commercial bank lending decisions. This stands in sharp contrast to former periods when banks paid little attention to the IMF, countries borrowed from banks to avoid going to the IMF, and banks would not have considered allowing the Fund to push them to make new loans.

Finally, the IMF has moved away from simply assessing the balance-of-payments consequences of adjustment policies. It has begun to develop a more microeconomic approach, encouraging policies directed at fundamental improvements in particular industries or sectors of the economy. It has developed early-warning procedures to signal a country's oncoming or increasing deficits. And it has regularized consultations with governments facing balance-of-payments problems—both to determine when to release new tranches of funding to them and to suggest policy changes that could avoid the need for additional balance-of-payments financing.

6

Reform of the Monetary System

The developing-country debt problem was one of the two major difficulties facing the world economy in the mid-1980s. The other was that of international exchange-rate misalignment and instability. As described in Chapter 4, the system of floating exchange rates was institutionalized by default. The inability to set credible and sustainable parities during the 1973 oil crisis convinced governments that a temporary, generalized float was necessary. For a variety of reasons the floating rate system has now lost a great deal of support—both abroad and in the United States itself.

First, as mentioned earlier, the floating rate system has been associated with great turbulence in currency markets. The dollar has proved especially volatile—its value moving from very low levels in the late 1970s to very high levels in the early 1980s, only to drop significantly in late 1985 and 1986. Its gyrations in this decade have necessitated painful adjustments for the United States and its trading partners. To be sure, some of the dollar's movements have reflected actual or anticipated changes in U.S. economic policies and performance as well as those of the world's other major economies. However, exchange rates have shown a marked tendency to move to extremes not justified by underlying economic conditions.

Although Article IV of the IMF charter commits countries to try to avoid currency volatility, little concerted effort was made to adjust currency rates until September 1985. One reason there were few credible attempts to manage currency rates was the widely held view that private individuals and institutions (such as banks, pension funds and insurance companies) held such large sums of money—far exceeding the amount of reserves of central banks—that they could overwhelm government intervention in currency markets.

The United States for years eschewed an active policy of managing currencies. The Reagan Administration did so with an especially ideological fervor, which convinced other nations that it was not interested in cooperation to manage currency problems. But exports and imports have become increasingly important to the U.S. economy—14 percent of GNP in 1986 as compared with roughly 7 percent two decades ago. Exports now account for 40 percent of U.S. sales of agricultural products, and most U.S. manufactured goods now face stiff international competition. Thus, stable and market-related exchange rates are now of greater importance to a larger number of Americans and to the factories, farms and offices in which they work than in past years. The increased significance of international trade to the United States underlies the increased interest in this country in improving the international monetary system.

A second, and related, reason for the greater U.S. concern about the international monetary system is the growing difference between the relative size of the U.S. economy and the dollar's role in the world economy. Total world GNP has increased more rapidly than the U.S. GNP over the years. Consequently the U.S. economy has become relatively less dominant in the world. Meanwhile the dollar continues to be by far the leading currency in which payments for international trade are made, international financial transactions are conducted, and nations hold their reserves. Therefore there is increased risk that dollar volatility—

billions of dollars are traded daily in international financial markets—will play havoc with the U.S. economy.

The Federal Reserve Board might be called upon to take more frequent measures to stabilize the value of the dollar in order to prevent sharp movements in that currency from disrupting the U.S. economy—even when such measures run counter to other domestic policy objectives. For example, at times the Fed might find itself under pressure to tighten domestic monetary policy to prevent a sharp decline in the dollar. The Fed might opt to increase interest rates and thereby slow or reverse any outflow of dollars that threatened to bring on a precipitous decline in the dollar's value in terms of foreign currencies. A steep decline could well bring on inflation because the dollar prices of U.S. imports would rise sharply in such a situation, and the prices of domestically made goods would follow. But a tighter monetary policy would weaken domestic demand in the United States when other considerations might argue against such a course.

A third reason is the tendency of financial and trade policies to conflict, with the real (goods) side of the economy at odds with the financial side. Manufacturers, farmers, importers, exporters and other participants in the economy have all too frequently seen sound investment and production decisions turn sour because of currency volatility over which they had little control and which they had little capacity to predict. Currency misalignments have on occasion wiped out the profits and undermined the sales of well run companies, and led to the layoffs of productive workers. In other circumstances undervalued currencies have subsidized companies and workers that could not have competed had their nations' currencies traded at more market-related rates. No system which cannot better contain such distortions can expect to retain public support for long.

A Summit for Exchange Rates

Concerns about the international monetary system in 1982 prompted the presidents and prime ministers of the major industrialized nations to discuss in some detail the problems of exchange rate instability at their eighth annual economic summit meeting, in Versailles, France. The United States argued that were there to be greater policy convergence leading to lower inflation, the long-sought currency stability would be achieved. France, with support from its European colleagues, expressed frustration with the inability of the United States to reduce its budget deficit and Washington's seemingly rigid opposition to exchange rate intervention. The Europeans argued that more exchange rate intervention could contribute to less turbulence in currency markets.

In the end, the leaders agreed both to study the effectiveness of government intervention in currency markets and to establish a multilateral surveillance group to encourage greater policy convergence. The group included the finance ministers of the five countries from whose currencies the value of the Special Drawing Right is derived—Britain, France, Japan, the United States and West Germany—plus the managing director of the IMF. The Group of Five has taken on a central role in the attempt to manage exchange rates.

The study on intervention was published prior to the next summit, in 1983 in Williamsburg, Virginia. It concluded that coordinated intervention could be effective in countering volatility in currency markets, but it also recognized that stability in those markets depends on a convergence of policies among the major economies. However, the United States continued its opposition to exchange rate intervention and managed to water down the Williamsburg communiqué on the subject to read, "We are willing to undertake coordinated intervention in exchange markets in instances where it is agreed that such intervention would be helpful." In effect, the leaders were saying that their countries would not intervene unless they wished to do so—a signal that markets saw as lukewarm at best.

The leaders at Williamsburg were more specific on the subject of surveillance. The Group of Five was mandated to work toward "policies designed to bring about greater convergence of economic performance" among their economies. To do the job, the countries in the group were urged to seek "disciplined noninflationary growth of monetary aggregates, and appropriate interest rates," to "reduce structural budget deficits," to "improve consultations, policy convergence, and international cooperation to help stabilize exchange markets," and to work toward "enhancing flexibility and openness of economies and financial markets; encouraging research and development" and "improved international cooperation . . . on structural adjustment measures. . . ."

Williamsburg summit participants also agreed to ask their finance ministers to join with the managing director of the IMF to "define the conditions for improving the international monetary system and to consider the part which might, in due course, be played in this process by a high-level international monetary conference." Such a conference had been urged by French President François Mitterrand, who had sought a "new Bretton Woods" to reform the international monetary system.

The finance ministers, in fulfilling their mandate to consider monetary reform, decided to use the already existing forum of the Group of Ten, and to include central bank governors in their deliberations. The ministers and governors in turn asked their deputies to prepare a report on "ways in which progressive improvements [in the international monetary system] may be sought." The deputies group, chaired by Lamberto Dini, the highly respected deputy governor of the Bank of Italy, completed its report in early 1985. It concluded that "the basic structure of the present system . . . has provided the essential flexibility for individual nations and the international community as a whole to respond constructively to a period of major adjustment to global change."

The deputies also agreed that "the fundamental approach of the Articles [of the IMF] remains valid and that the key elements of the current international monetary system require no major institutional change." The deputies recognized, however, that the system had also "shown weakness and that there is a need to improve its functioning in order to foster greater stability by promoting convergence of economic performances through the adoption of sound and compatible policies in IMF member countries." They emphasized that "an essential condition of exchange rate stability is convergence of economic performance in the direction of sustainable noninflationary growth." That, in turn, "requires not only sound, consistent policies but also the removal of artificial barriers and structural rigidities which inhibit market flexibility." The IMF, the deputies group notes, was given responsibility by Article IV to exercise "surveillance over the exchange rate policies in order to ensure that members fulfill their obligations, *inter alia*, to: i) pursue economic and financial policies aimed at orderly economic growth with reasonable price stability; ii) foster underlying economic and financial conditions that do not tend to produce erratic disruptions."

Strong Surveillance

While recognizing that the Fund had been developing experience in exercising its surveillance responsibilities, the report recommended a number of ways to strengthen the process. These included greater involvement of senior-level officials of major countries, increasing public scrutiny of economic performance, encouraging governments to take the advice of other nations (and the need for international adjustment) into account in making policy decisions, as well as a greater role for the IMF managing director in the surveillance process.

The deputies also recognized that some variability is inherent in freely floating exchange rates. That same point was echoed in the IMF's 1985 *Annual Report* which noted that "it is often difficult to know what the appropriate policy measures are" to promote adjustment. Moreover, the report added, "it is not always clear whether an exchange rate movement is the consequence of a shift in currency preferences or of more fundamental developments." On a more basic level, politicians and business people alike found it difficult to convince themselves that surveillance could be a strong enough instrument to correct the large U.S. current account deficit and a grossly overvalued dollar.

Because the suggested improvements in the IMF surveillance process were seen as a medium-term goal and were not expected to bring about immediate policy changes sufficient to produce a major currency realignment, other approaches were pursued.

Promising steps toward restoring a better alignment of curren-

Oswaldo/Excelsior/Mexico City © 1987 Cartoonists & Writers Syndicate

cies in the near term were taken by the Group of Five. In September 1985 Treasury Secretary Baker, Fed Chairman Volcker, and their counterparts from Britain, France, Japan and West Germany, recognizing that the dollar's then extraordinary strength was distorting international trade and financial flows—and risking protectionist legislation in the U.S. Congress—agreed that "exchange rates should better reflect fundamental economic conditions than has been the case" and that "further orderly appreciation of the main nondollar currencies against the dollar is desirable." They pledged to "cooperate more closely to encourage this."

The United States thus departed from its previous position of intervening in international currency markets only to counter extremely disorderly conditions; it now agreed also to intervene in a situation in which currencies did not reflect underlying economic realities. The U.S. shift marked a sharp break with the practice of uncoordinated floating and a major step toward greater management of the floating rate system.

The new agreement, reached at the Plaza Hotel in New York City, was largely based on political considerations: it was a constructive effort by the United States and its trading partners to forestall new legislation in the U.S. Congress to restrict imports. In addition, it served to bring greater order to the international monetary system. The agreement was reached at a time when forces in foreign exchange markets, and changes in U.S. and other countries' domestic policies, were already moving in directions that tended to lower the dollar's value. The U.S. commitment to bring about a further decline in the dollar, because of this, was considered by currency markets to be credible. For example, an easier monetary policy by the Fed was anticipated as a measure to revive a sluggish American economy by lowering U.S. interest rates.

The Plaza accord gave impetus to the appreciation of the yen and the West German mark and the decline of the dollar. Although the improvement in the U.S. trade position came only very slowly after the dollar's fall, the change in currency rates was seen as part of the necessary adjustment process. The agreement's significance was correctly cited by Deutsche Bundesbank President Karl Otto Pöhl as "the beginning of close cooperation and coordination of economic and monetary policies." But over time, concerns emerged (especially in Western Europe and Japan) that the dollar was in danger of "overshooting" on the downside. A second major Group of Five agreement, at the Louvre, Paris, in early 1987, sought to stem the dollar's drop by stressing that "further substantial exchange rate shifts among currencies could damage growth and adjustment prospects in all countries." Participants "agreed to cooperate closely to foster stability of exchange rates around current levels."

The dollar's prolonged strength and its extraordinary volatility helped to focus attention on the subject of monetary reform. Many Americans in the early 1980s, as in 1971, argued that the international monetary system worked to the disadvantage of the United States and pressures thus emerged for changes in the system. In other nations pressures for systemic change arose because of concerns over currency volatility and, more recently, the dollar's sharp decline.

It must, however, be added that the desire for improving the monetary system is greater than the degree of consensus on how it should be improved.

In a more fundamental sense, what reform has taken place of late has been undertaken by the private sector. New techniques such as currency swaps, an active currency futures and options market, and various other sophisticated hedging concepts have arisen in response to currency volatility and the desire of corporations and financial institutions to avert the attendant economic and financial risks. These techniques have cushioned the impact of currency turmoil for some, although prolonged misalignments cannot easily be offset by such devices. Nonetheless, the existence of ways to avert currency risk have to a degree reduced the urgency of monetary reform in the eyes of some observers.

Prospects for Change and Reform

In coming years a wide range of techniques for stabilizing currencies will be explored. A number of plans now under consideration, and doubtless many variations, will be debated and examined under monetary microscopes. In any case, monetary reform is likely to be a slow process, carefully pursued. It is not a matter to be embarked upon lightly because it can profoundly affect the lives of a considerable portion of the world's population and every aspect of economic life on this planet. Leaders can now blame some of their nations' economic ills on the present system, which they inherited; they will bear a greater share of the blame for difficulties stemming from any new system created by governments over which they preside.

Many economic officials recognize that, even assuming the best of intent, a more stable system will be difficult to restore. The stability of the fixed-but-adjustable Bretton Woods system was in part possible because governments were in possession of much of the world's liquidity, and stability was often maintained through the use of capital controls. But recent liberalization of capital markets and the introduction of new technologies that permit the virtually instantaneous transmission of information and funds have given capital enormous international mobility and made its movement more difficult for governments to control than ever before. The volume of international capital transactions has grown dramatically since 1972, the last full year in which governments tried to maintain fixed exchange rates. In that year the volume of international syndicated lending was $7 billion; in 1985 it amounted to roughly $55 billion. In 1972 total Eurocurrency deposits amounted to about $200 billion; the total is now over $3 trillion.

Countries are increasingly dependent on international capital markets to obtain funds needed to finance domestic investment, consumption and budget deficits. And investors are becoming increasingly accustomed to the returns and diversification obtainable in world capital markets. At the same time, attempts to limit capital flows in order to manipulate exchange rates would doubtless cause gross distortions in the major economies. Such attempts would cause interest rates to rise in countries that limit the inflow of capital, thereby hurting domestic business; and cause interest rates to fall in countries that limit the outflow of capital, thereby giving their domestic businesses an artificial incentive to borrow and a cooperative edge in capital costs.

However, because trade today accounts for a larger portion of GNP in most nations than it did 10 years ago, governments regard stable and properly aligned currency rates as more important than ever. Nevertheless, many governments are reluctant to agree permanently to subordinate other domestic policy objectives to the goal of keeping currencies fixed in some preestablished alignment. And even should governments adopt exchange rate stability as a single-minded objective, they may not be able to achieve it. As Hannes Androsch, chairman of Austria's Creditanstalt Bankverein, and Toyoo Gyohten, Japan's vice minister of finance, observed at a 1986 conference, a nation's exchange rate is a reflection of its entire state of affairs—financial, military, diplomatic and sometimes cultural. Simply making changes in economic policy will not always be enough to keep currencies in line.

The Fundamental Question

All this does not mean that greater stability cannot be attained. Increasingly, the stability and the proper alignment of currency rates has come to be recognized as important to the prosperity of the world's economies and to the promotion of orderly movements of goods and capital. President Ronald Reagan's change of position on this question illustrates the degree to which he has recognized the impact of currency misalignments on the U.S. economy. Early in his Administration he regarded the strong dollar as a positive development—a sign of foreign confidence in the U.S. economy. His attitude toward the dollar at that time was to welcome its strength; he seemed little concerned about, indeed oblivious to, a strong dollar's effects on U.S. industry and agriculture. In a dramatic change of view, his 1986 State of the Union address emphasized that "the constant expansion of our economy and exports requires a sound and stable dollar at home and reliable exchange rates around the world. We must never again permit world currency swings to cripple our farmers and other exporters. . . . I am directing Treasury Secretary Jim Baker to determine if the nations of the world should convene to discuss the role and relationships of our currencies." That speech gave rise to a more vigorous debate in the United States as to whether international monetary reform was needed and, if so, what kind would achieve the desired results.

Since that address, however, there has been growing evidence that simply tinkering with the exchange rate system alone will not produce currency stability or proper currency alignments, and that exchange rate changes alone will not lead to an improved balance-of-payments equilibrium. There has been growing recognition that reform of the international monetary system is perhaps too narrow a way of looking at the issue. The more fundamental question is whether there can be a reform in attitudes of governments sufficient to ensure that domestic policies will be aimed to a greater degree at avoiding major international disequilibria.

Fixed exchange rates, floating rates within a preset zone or band, or exchange rates linked to some real good (such as gold) or group of real goods (such as a basket of commodities) have been suggested as ways of imposing greater discipline on domestic economic policy. (See the Appendix.)

As yet no consensus has emerged around such proposals. Governments have instead focused their attention on less bold schemes which have evolved from discussions about improved "multilateral surveillance" and the pragmatic cooperation and coordination displayed at the Plaza and the Louvre. The debate has concentrated on ways to monitor and modify domestic policies in order to avoid incompatibilities in fiscal and monetary policies that can lead to currency and trade misalignments. Improved surveillance and efforts to enhance cooperation have not proved particularly successful in, for instance, convincing the United States to reduce its large budget deficit that draws in foreign capital, or in inducing countries with large current account surpluses to stimulate their economies in order to import more. Nevertheless, that approach appears to be for the moment the one around which there is greatest international consensus.

Finance ministers and central bank governors have concluded that improved harmony in underlying economic policies and conditions is less difficult to attain than progress in reforming the international monetary system. Thus the discussions among governments to date have not been about currency reform per se but about domestic policy compatibility.

A Forward Step in Tokyo

An important step toward improving the procedural basis for policy harmonization was taken at the Tokyo economic summit in May 1986. The finance ministers of the seven countries participating in the summit were requested, in conjunction with the managing director of the IMF, "to review their individual economic objectives and forecasts collectively at least once a year, using indicators specified in the communiqué, with a particular view to examining their mutual compatibility." Such indicators would include "GNP growth rates, inflation rates, interest rates, unemployment rates, fiscal deficit ratios, current account and trade balances, monetary growth rates, reserves, and exchange rates." Governments would "make their best efforts to reach an understanding on appropriate remedial measures whenever there are significant deviations from an intended course; and recommend that remedial efforts focus first and foremost on underlying policy fundamentals, while reaffirming the 1983 Williamsburg commitment to intervene in exchange markets when to do so would be helpful."

"What is new in the arrangements adopted in Tokyo," in the words of Secretary Baker, "is that the major industrial countries have agreed that their economic forecasts and objectives will be specified, taking into account a broad range of indicators, and their internal consistency and external compatibility will be assessed. Moreover, if there are inconsistencies, efforts will be made to achieve necessary adjustments so that the forecasts and objectives of the key currencies will mesh. Finally, if economic performance falls short of an intended course, it is explicitly agreed that countries will use their best efforts to reach understanding regarding appropriate corrective action."

It remains to be seen how well this system of "indicators" will work out, or whether governments will actually take the "corrective action" needed to put them back on course should their performance "fall short of an intended course." However, until this process is given a chance to work, it is unlikely that the more elaborate changes in the monetary system currently under discussion will be tried. Moreover the Tokyo summit procedures will test the willingness of governments to modify economic policies if they fail to conform to the indicators. If they are willing to do so, prospects for a more elaborate reform of the monetary system may be improved, although reform may become less necessary. If they are not willing to make policy changes, governments will need to consider seriously whether they wish to impose tougher, and less discretionary, external constraints on their policies in order to foster improved international economic equilibrium. The grounds would be that such constraints could be invoked to convince populations to support domestic policy changes because they were mandated by external "rules." Past experience makes this a very dubious proposition although, were a major crisis in the international monetary system to occur, support for tighter rules could grow dramatically.

Tests and Trade-offs

In any case, the test of any new system will necessarily be in the political, economic and financial marketplaces. The political test will turn on whether domestic leaders and legislatures in the large industrialized countries, and their populations, will see the system as promoting their general well-being, and whether the groups with the greatest influence in these matters will support it. Nearly all of the ideas for improving the monetary system require countries to give up a bit of their economic sovereignty in order to foster a better functioning world economy—which, in turn, should make them better off. But, having said that, it must be admitted that such policy trade-offs are difficult. In a democracy it is hard enough to make *domestic* policy trade-offs on economic issues. Taking policies arduously worked out at home, renegotiating them abroad, and then generating domestic support for them will be tougher still. Such a process will only work if countries recognize that an international strategy to achieve a better functioning world economy is so important to their long-term economic well-being that they should make short-term policy changes in order to contribute to that strategy. And even then each country will evaluate the immediate costs and benefits of its "concessions" to be sure that it did not give up more than others or obtain fewer advantages.

Economically, the test will center on whether the system can restore greater confidence among traders, manufacturers, workers and investors in regard to currency stability. No system which plays havoc with these major economic players will long enjoy their support.

There has in the past been a remarkable lack of dialogue within governments between officials responsible for specific trade and business policies and those responsible for overall economic and monetary policies. Moreover, the business community is rarely consulted on international monetary issues vital to it. These gaps within the government and between the government and the business community must be closed in an era in which currency rates can spell the success or failure of a domestic investment, a foreign investment, or indeed any major transaction.

July 1986: Tokyo currency brokers busy at work dealing with their customers as the dollar falls to a new low of 158 yen

Cross-purposes or Concord?

Financially, the test will be whether the system can convince participants in currency markets and capital markets that governments are in fact going to work more closely to avoid incompatible domestic policies. If governments appear to be acting at cross-purposes, currency market disorder is likely to plague the system. In particular it must be recognized that, unlike the two decades after the Bretton Woods agreements when governments were the dominant actors, today the private sector is the principal player in the international currency market. The financial community will need to be brought in on major discussions involving the monetary system in order to provide an evaluation of how changes will actually work.

Predictions about the future of the international monetary system are difficult to make at this point. Whether the Tokyo formula will take hold or some other approach will be tried is unclear at the time of this writing. What does appear likely is that if greater currency stability cannot be achieved, there will be pressure to control capital movements in order to dampen the volatility of currencies. And legislatures will attempt to restrict trade to offset economic distortions caused by misaligned currencies. Steps of this nature would be a setback to all economies. They would raise precisely the sorts of political and security questions that concerned President Roosevelt and his secretary of state, as noted in the first chapter.

And so we have come full circle. In the final analysis the international monetary system has a political and security dimension as well as an economic and financial one. Countries constantly at odds about exchange rates make bad trading partners and bad allies. There appears to be growing awareness of such an incompatibility in the United States and among its economic partners. Whether that awareness can be translated into genuine improvements in economic and monetary cooperation will be critical to all of our futures.

APPENDIX

Several types of formal proposals have been put forward for improving or reforming the international monetary system.

Target Zones

Advocates of target zones, such as C. Fred Bergsten and John Williamson of the Institute for International Economics and Robert V. Roosa of Brown Brothers Harriman, see the concept as a device for better management of currencies without imposing excessive rigidities on the system. Under such a plan, governments would agree on target values for their currencies and on zones around them within which these currencies could fluctuate. They would undertake to prevent their currencies from moving outside of these zones.

Williamson's proposal would set a "fundamental equilibrium exchange rate," one which in the best judgment of monetary officials would lead to balance in the current accounts of the major economies. Monetary policy would be employed—interest rates would be raised or lowered—to keep a country's currency within the target zone, which could be up to 20 percent in width, 10 percent above or below the central rate. However, in Williamson's words, a "country's authorities retain the right to allow their internal objectives to override their exchange rate targets even in the event of a large misalignment." Williamson's concept of an override suggests that the zone would have "soft margins" and takes into account the probability that the United States, among others, would not want to be locked into a permanent commitment to give priority at all times to exchange rate objectives over domestic monetary or interest rate objectives. Williamson's proposals are among the most highly developed of the new ideas for reforming the monetary system and would not require the more dramatic changes envisaged by a number of others.

A target-zone concept of a similar nature was also proposed by a number of the Group of Ten deputies. The proposal discussed by the deputies called for a progressive phasing in of the target zones. The zones would provide a framework for triggering consultations that "would induce, step by step, more direct links between domestic policies and exchange rate considerations." The scheme would not, according to its advocates in the group, necessarily involve rigid commitments to intervene in foreign exchange markets.

Critics of target-zone proposals question whether agreement could be reached on central currency rates and whether the scheme avoids the ambiguities in the Bretton Woods system concerning how to determine whether, in the event of a disagreement, it is the country in balance-of-payments surplus or the country in payments deficit that should adjust. Critics of a phased approach might argue that its defects would be similar to those of target zones, although the fact that this proposal would ease into reference zones (see below) might reduce concerns that agreed rates would be difficult to set. Other questions would relate to the degree to which such zones could be convincing to domestic populations as a reason for taking unpopular policy-adjustment measures.

Many of the deputies concluded that "reaching a consensus on the range of desirable exchange rates would prove extremely difficult." They also noted that "given our imperfect knowledge of the determinants of exchange rate movements, the target zones would have to be too wide to serve as an anchor for expectations." The majority of the deputies agreed that "the adoption of target zones is undesirable and in any case impractical in current circumstances." It must be noted, however, that circumstances have changed since the report was issued and support may have grown somewhat since that time.

Reference Zones (French Proposal)

France, long a major participant in international currency debates, has suggested establishing a less rigid variant of target zones, namely reference zones. Under the plan proposed by Daniel Lebeque, director of the French Treasury, officials would first agree on a set of exchange rates for the principal currencies, accompanied by a "range of uncertainty" around each value. Countries would ease into the rates and ranges on the basis of arrangements which are compatible with a pattern of balance-of-payments stability. These might first be set on an empirical basis and formalized later on the basis of work done by finance ministers and central bank governors. There would be a range of policy measures to help countries to maintain their currencies within these zones. Such measures could range from a simple statement of firmness of purpose to domestic policy shifts.

Lebeque also points to the need to diversify currency holdings. He suggests that the United States finance part of its borrowings in foreign currencies and that the IMF make better use of the SDR. The IMF, he believes, should more actively monitor international liquidity, perhaps using SDR assets at the margin to expand global liquidity.

Criticisms of this proposal are similar to those of target zones, and the benefits would be similar as well.

Commodity-Anchored Target Zones

Under this scheme, target zones would be anchored by a basket, or group, of primary commodities or other real goods. The center of the zone for a country would be linked to a basket of products. For example, the dollar might equal some portion of the value of a blend of 10 bushels of wheat, one half ton of tin, one half ton of copper, 10 bushels of soybeans and an ounce of gold. If the dollar deviated too much from its previously established relationship to the basket, the United States would take steps to bring its currency closer to the center of its zone. For instance, a sharp rise in the cost of the basket in dollars (indicating a decline in the dollar's relative purchasing power) could be a sign to the U.S. government to tighten up on domestic monetary policy in order to raise the value of the dollar in relation to the basket. Variants would include linking only a few of the major currencies to the basket of commodities, while other currencies float in some band vis-à-vis the major ones. Or—in principle, at least—all currencies could be linked to a basket. Or the SDR could be pegged to a basket, with currencies floating in a zone around the SDR.

Such proposals are predicated on the notion that it is more desirable to peg currencies to a group of real goods with their own intrinsic value than to other currencies that are created by governments and whose values depend on their acceptability in exchange for goods, services and investments. Product-anchored target zones might, therefore, help to answer the question: When there is a major imbalance between a surplus and deficit country, is it the surplus or the deficit country that should adjust and by how much?

Critics argue that commodity prices could change as the result of natural forces, such as the failure of the U.S. soybean crop, political instability affecting South African gold mines, or a tin strike in Bolivia. Such events would play havoc with international monetary policies based on keeping currencies aligned with a basket of commodities. And, as in the target-zone plan, there would be problems in determining the original central rates.

Advocates of some type of product-based system include Ronald McKinnon of Stanford University and Alexander Swoboda of the Institut Universitaire de Hautes Etudes Internationales in Geneva.

Gold-Anchored Target Zones

There are several ways a gold-anchored target zone might work. The United States could once again fix the dollar in terms of gold while other currencies move in some zone vis-à-vis the dollar. Or the major economies could all fix their exchange rates in terms of the market value of gold and permit their currencies to float in some band around that rate. Or the SDR could be fixed in terms of gold and be the center of the zone. In the latter case, each major economy would agree to make its currency convertible into SDRs and thus implicitly into gold.

As in the case of a deviation from central rates in any system using zones, a significant divergence from a country's gold parity, or anchor, would create an a priori case for adjustment, which is likely to be a loosening or tightening of a country's monetary policy. Proper central bank control over domestic monetary policies could also reduce the movement of the immense amounts of currently highly mobile international currencies. Some schemes propose a narrow zone; others propose a broad zone.

Critics charge that gold is too volatile a commodity to link currencies to. And, as with all the foregoing schemes, the volatility of international capital would make the stability promised by the gold link difficult to attain. Moreover, the deputies' criticism of all target zones would apply to this one: "the constraints imposed on domestic policies by target zones might undermine efforts to pursue sound and stable policies in a medium-term framework." Supporters of the gold-centered system would counter that these are precisely the policy objectives that such a system would promote. Robert Mundell of Columbia University, Congressman Jack Kemp (R-N.Y.) and Lewis Lehrman, a New York business-man and political figure, are advocates of systems with a strong gold anchor.

A Globalized European Monetary System

A proposal to globalize the European Monetary System would work in much the same way as the current EMS. The EMS, as noted above, operates on the basis of an agreed zone which limits the deviation of EMS currencies among themselves. EMS currencies can be realigned from time to time when market conditions make it impossible to maintain existing central rates. Currencies are denominated in terms of ECUs, the European Currency Unit.

To globalize this type of system, the EMS scheme would have to be revamped to contain a new mixture of currencies; and the United States and Japan would need to accept a major commit-ment to modify their domestic policies and to intervene coopera-tively in currency markets to ensure greater stability. Critics point out that the EMS might work for Western Europe, because its economies are so closely interlinked. Its governments recognize the internal costs of currency volatility and misalignments and therefore will normally modify domestic policies to avoid them. Some members utilize capital controls to discourage volatile capital movements. Other large economies are less closely linked and less inclined, especially the United States, to use capital controls or to modify domestic policies for international reasons.

An International Monetary Stabilization Account

Proposed by Takashi Hosomi, former vice minister of finance for international affairs of Japan, this scheme calls for the United States, West Germany and Japan to put a certain amount of capital in their national currencies into a common account—the International Monetary Stabilization Account. The IMSA could issue securities, denominated in dollars, deutsche marks and yen, backed by this capital. The funds generated by the sale of these securities would be invested in assets denominated in such currencies. If one or more of these currencies deviate from an agreed zone, or, as Hosomi puts it, enter a "negative zone," the portfolio of IMSA assets would be shifted around to stabilize rates. Thus, the IMSA would buy and sell securities to stabilize currencies much as the Federal Reserve seeks to influence interest rates by buying and selling U.S. Treasury securities. It is, in effect, a plan for large-scale joint intervention. The centralized stabilization effort would, in its author's view, have a significant impact on the market. The account would be run through direct negotiations among the monetary authorities of the three countries.

Critics of this proposal raise concerns that West Germany would not be able to participate in this system if its responsibilities were in conflict with its role in the EMS. They also argue that it gives insufficient attention to coordination of underlying economic policies, and that countries might not be willing to give up as much control over intervention as this scheme requires. This proposal would represent a step, if only a small one, toward a world central bank and would probably be more convincing to markets than ad hoc or uncoordinated intervention. □

Talking It Over

A Note for Students and Discussions Groups

This issue of the HEADLINE SERIES, like its predecessors, is published for every serious reader, specialized or not, who takes an interest in the subject. Many of our readers will be in classrooms, seminars or community discussion groups. Particularly with them in mind, we present below some discussion questions—suggested as a starting point only—and references for further reading.

Discussion Questions

In light of the recent turmoil in currency markets, should policymakers seek major reform of the international monetary system or the fundamentals of domestic policy? Or can progress on the former lead to progress on the latter?

To what extent should the IMF and World Bank work more closely together? Is there a danger that their missions will become less clear if their work overlaps too much?

If there were no IMF or World Bank, what might the international economy look like? Would America's economic or security interests be better or less-well served in such a world?

Over the longer run, should the international monetary system remain very flexible as it is today, or should there be some effort to establish and maintain agreed parities or targets?

Has the IMF played a helpful role in dealing with the Latin American debt problem? What suggestions would you make to the IMF for addressing the debt problem in the future?

Has the United States given sufficient support to the IMF and World Bank? Would it be in the U.S. interest to give more support?

READING LIST

Gardner, Richard N., *Sterling-Dollar Diplomacy in Current Perspective: The Origins and the Prospects of Our International Economic Order*. New York, Columbia University Press, 1980. The definitive work on U.S.-British economic relationships and how the two countries built the postwar economic system.

Kenen, Peter B., "The Role of the Dollar as an International Currency," *Occasional Paper* 13. New York, The Group of Thirty, 1983. An incisive analysis of the multiple roles played by the dollar in the world economy and its enormous impact on trade and capital flows.

Mayer, Martin, *The Fate of the Dollar*. New York, Times Books, 1980. A penetrating behind-the-scenes look at international finance and how things happen in the international economy.

McKinnon, Ronald I., *An International Standard for Monetary Stabilization*. Washington, D.C., Institute for International Economics, 1984. Describes the need for nations to work together to stabilize the purchasing power of their currencies through control of their aggregate money stock.

Solomon, Robert, *The International Monetary System, 1945-1981*. New York, Harper & Row, 1982. The single best history of the international monetary system, by one who participated intimately in the making of that history.

Spero, Joan Edelman, *The Politics of International Economic Relations*, 3rd ed. New York, St. Martin's Press, 1985. A well written and very thorough analysis of the history and underlying causes of recent developments in the world economy.

Williamson, John, *The Exchange Rate System*, 2nd ed. Washington, D.C., Institute for International Economics, 1985. The best description of and argument in behalf of target zones.

GLOSSARY

balance of payments: A record of all economic transactions that take place between a country and the rest of the world, usually measured annually.

balance of trade (merchandise): The difference between the value of the goods a nation imports and the value of the goods it exports. Unlike the balance of payments, it doesn't include payments for services and capital transactions.

band: See p. 21.

basket of currency: Several currencies combined in order to reduce fluctuations that could occur with a single currency. A basket is usually weighted—strong currencies make up a larger percentage of the basket's value than weaker currencies.

beggar-thy-neighbor policies: Government strategies to improve domestic situations at the expense of other countries. For example, restrictions on trade to help domestic producers would hurt foreign producers.

Committee of Twenty: See p. 33.

convertibility: A currency is convertible when it can be exchanged for another currency. See also p. 8.

current account: The part of the balance of payments that measures exports and imports of goods and services. See also p. 8.

devaluation: The lowering by a government of the value of its currency in terms of the currencies of other nations. Revaluation is when a government raises the value of its currency vis-à-vis other currencies.

discount rate: The interest the Federal Reserve charges commercial banks that borrow from Federal Reserve banks.

ECU: See p. 41.

EEC: The European Economic Community, also called the Common Market, is the main element in the European Communities (the others are the European Atomic Energy Community or Euratom and the European Coal and Steel Community). Its members are France, the Federal Republic of Germany, Italy, Belgium, the Netherlands, Luxembourg, Britain, Denmark, Ireland, Greece, Spain and Portugal. The EEC was established by the first six countries in 1958.

Eurocurrency: Money (e.g. dollar, yen) held outside its country of origin and used in European money markets.

European Monetary System: See p. 40.

exchange rate: The price of one nation's currency in terms of another nation's currency.

fixed exchange rate, parity rate: See p. 7 and p. 21.

float, floating exchange rate: The price of a currency determined by supply and demand on the free market. See also p. 16 and p. 23.

fundamental disequilibrium: See p. 8.

General Arrangements to Borrow: See p. 15.

gold pool: See p. 13.

gross national product (GNP): The total value of all final goods and services produced by a nation's economy.

Group of Five: See p. 56.

Group of Ten: The original members are Belgium, Britain, Canada, France, Federal Republic of Germany, Italy, Japan, the Netherlands, Sweden and the United States. Switzerland joined in 1983. See also p. 15.

IMF conditionality: See p. 43.

IMF quota: See p. 18.

Interim Committee: See p. 38.

intervention in currency markets: See p. 8.

liquidity: A measure of a country's liquid assets—currency plus any holding that can be quickly converted to cash without great loss.

reserve indicator: See p. 35.

snake, snake in tunnel: See p. 30.

soft loan: Low-interest long-term loans given by the International Development Association (IDA) to developing countries. See p. 48.

Special Drawing Rights, SDRs (sometimes called paper gold): System of reserve currency created in 1969 by members of the International Monetary Fund. SDRs are allocated among countries according to their shares in the IMF and may be transferred within the IMF to obtain other currencies. See pp. 17–18.

speculation: See p. 10.

standby agreement: See p. 43.

tranche: See p. 42.

zone: See band, p. 21.

U.S. Postal Service

STATEMENT OF OWNERSHIP, MANAGEMENT AND CIRCULATION
Required by 39 U.S.C. 3685)

1A. TITLE OF PUBLICATION	1B. PUBLICATION NO.									2. DATE OF FILING
HEADLINE SERIES	0	0	1	7	8	7	8	0		12/15/86

3. FREQUENCY OF ISSUE	3A. NO. OF ISSUES PUBLISHED ANNUALLY	3B. ANNUAL SUBSCRIPTION PRICE
January, March, May, September, November	5	$ 15.00

4. COMPLETE MAILING ADDRESS OF KNOWN OFFICE OF PUBLICATION *(Street, City, County, State and ZIP+4 Code) (Not printers)*

FOREIGN POLICY ASSOCIATION, 205 Lexington Avenue, New York, N.Y. 10016

5. COMPLETE MAILING ADDRESS OF THE HEADQUARTERS OF GENERAL BUSINESS OFFICES OF THE PUBLISHER *(Not printer)*

Same as above

6. FULL NAMES AND COMPLETE MAILING ADDRESS OF PUBLISHER, EDITOR, AND MANAGING EDITOR *(This item MUST NOT be blank)*

PUBLISHER *(Name and Complete Mailing Address)*

FOREIGN POLICY ASSOCIATION, 205 Lexington Avenue, New York, N.Y. 10016

EDITOR *(Name and Complete Mailing Address)*

Nancy Hoepli, address same as above.

MANAGING EDITOR *(Name and Complete Mailing Address)*

None

7. OWNER *(If owned by a corporation, its name and address must be stated and also immediately thereunder the names and addresses of stockholders owning or holding 1 percent or more of total amount of stock. If not owned by a corporation, the names and addresses of the individual owners must be given. If owned by a partnership or other unincorporated firm, its name and address, as well as that of each individual must be given. If the publication is published by a nonprofit organization, its name and address must be stated.) (Item must be completed.)*

FULL NAME	COMPLETE MAILING ADDRESS
FOREIGN POLICY ASSOCIATION	205 Lexington Avenue, New York NY 10016

8. KNOWN BONDHOLDERS, MORTGAGEES, AND OTHER SECURITY HOLDERS OWNING OR HOLDING 1 PERCENT OR MORE OF TOTAL AMOUNT OF BONDS, MORTGAGES OR OTHER SECURITIES *(If there are none, so state)*

FULL NAME	COMPLETE MAILING ADDRESS
No stockholders - a nonprofit organization	

9. FOR COMPLETION BY NONPROFIT ORGANIZATIONS AUTHORIZED TO MAIL AT SPECIAL RATES *(Section 423.12 DMM only)* The purpose, function, and nonprofit status of this organization and the exempt status for Federal income tax purposes *(Check one)*

(1) [X] HAS NOT CHANGED DURING PRECEDING 12 MONTHS   (2) [ ] HAS CHANGED DURING PRECEDING 12 MONTHS   *(If changed, publisher must submit explanation of change with this statement.)*

10. EXTENT AND NATURE OF CIRCULATION *(See instructions on reverse side)*	AVERAGE NO. COPIES EACH ISSUE DURING PRECEDING 12 MONTHS	ACTUAL NO. COPIES OF SINGLE ISSUE PUBLISHED NEAREST TO FILING DATE
A. TOTAL NO. COPIES *(Net Press Run)*	15,249	14,736
B. PAID AND/OR REQUESTED CIRCULATION 1. Sales through dealers and carriers, street vendors and counter sales	590	214
2. Mail Subscription *(Paid and/or requested)*	5,899	5,338
C. TOTAL PAID AND/OR REQUESTED CIRCULATION *(Sum of 10B1 and 10B2)*	6,489	5,552
D. FREE DISTRIBUTION BY MAIL, CARRIER OR OTHER MEANS SAMPLES, COMPLIMENTARY, AND OTHER FREE COPIES	500	500
E. TOTAL DISTRIBUTION *(Sum of C and D)*	6,989	6,052
F. COPIES NOT DISTRIBUTED 1. Office use, left over, unaccounted, spoiled after printing	8,260	8,684
2. Return from News Agents	-0-	-0-
G. TOTAL *(Sum of E, F1 and 2 - should equal net press run shown in A)*	15,249	14,736

11. I certify that the statements made by me above are correct and complete

SIGNATURE AND TITLE OF EDITOR, PUBLISHER, BUSINESS MANAGER OR OWNER

Director of ADministration

PS Form 3526, July 1984